GARY LIBRARY
VERMONT COLLEGE
36 COLLEGE STREET
MONTPELIER, VT 05602

WITHDRAWN

Please remember that this is a library book,
and that it belongs only temporarily to each
person who uses it. Be considerate. Do
not write in this, or any, library book.

Please remember that this is a library book,
and that it belongs only temporarily to each
person who uses it. Be considerate. Do
not write in this, or any, library book.

WITHDRAWN

ALSO BY EILEEN SIMPSON

The Maze (novel)
Poets in Their Youth: A Memoir
Orphans: Real and Imaginary
Late Love: A Celebration of Marriage after Fifty

Reversals

Reversals

A Personal Account of
Victory over Dyslexia

Eileen Simpson

THE NOONDAY PRESS
Farrar, Straus and Giroux
New York

/3.00

The Noonday Press
A division of Farrar, Straus and Giroux
19 Union Square West, New York 10003

Copyright © 1979, 1991 by Eileen Simpson
All rights reserved
Printed in the United States of America
Distributed in Canada by Douglas & McIntyre Ltd.
First published in 1979 by Houghton Mifflin Company
This revised edition first published in 1991 by The Noonday Press
Second printing, 1998

The Library of Congress has catalogued the hardcover edition as follows:
Simpson, Eileen B.
    Reversals : a personal account of victory over dyslexia / Eileen
    Simpson. — Rev. ed.
        p.   cm.
    Includes bibliographical references.
    ISBN 0-374-52316-9 : $9.95
        1. Simpson, Eileen B.—Health.   2. Dyslexics—United States—
    Biography.   I. Title.
    RC394.W6S55   1991
    362.1'968553'0092—dc20
    [B]   91-19839

For Marie

_____

Preface to the Noonday Edition

One of the inhibitions I had to overcome in writing *Reversals* was the fear that if I exposed my shady academic past and the limitations under which I continued to operate as a result of my incurable disability, I would be patronized by people in my milieu who as children had learned to read precociously, and as adults had developed exceptional linguistic facility. To my surprise, that did not happen. Instead, so many of them told me they knew someone — a cousin, a nephew — whose early school difficulties mimicked mine that I began to wonder if the statistics on the number of dyslexics in the population had not been underestimated.

In the year following publication, I received letters from fellow sufferers who said I had told their story. They, too, had had an agonizing time learning to read; they, too, had been thought to be stupid, or had been called lazy. Some still could not read, and wondered if at age forty, fifty, or sixty it was too late to learn. Others wrote about their heartbreak over a child, usually a son, who had begun by being a non-reader and was now a behavior problem. All of them complained about how difficult it was to find help.

Now, ten years later, they would not have the same complaint. The Orton Dyslexia Society, which in 1979 had twenty branches in the United States, today has forty-four. It also has a hot line (see page 243) one can call for referrals. The increase in the Society's size is reflected in a similar increase in remedial teachers. More and more elementary schools now spot children who are likely to have trouble learning to read before reading lessons begin, and see to it that they have special training (although one still hears of those who were not caught until the upper grades). Adults who for years had hidden their illiteracy are now joining others in groups for support and remediation.

Remedial techniques for use with all age groups continue to be refined. The computer, which corrects errors without the censoriousness dyslexics used to be subjected to by their fellow students ("That's the fifth time you got that wrong!") and their teachers ("You're not trying"), has proved a boon to many. Increasingly, preparatory schools and colleges make special arrangements for dyslexics. There are also more special schools and colleges for those who, though bright, would not be able to compete with normal students.

Research on the neurophysiology of the brain, after years in the doldrums, has become an exciting field, thanks to the development of sophisticated machines — notably MRI (magnetic resonance imagery) and PET (positive emission typography) — that make possible detailed photographs of the living brain. Through these images, Dr. Albert Galaburda and others at the National Dyslexia Research Foundation are pinpointing nodules that perform highly specialized functions in processing language. They have confirmed what Orton suspected, that a dyslexic's brain is different, both in form and in function, from those of normal subjects.

As I listened to Dr. Galaburda present a paper at a recent meeting of the New York Orton Society on the work he is doing at NDRF, and saw his slides of a dyslexic's brain, with its two hemispheres of equal size (instead of a smaller right side, as in the brain of a normal subject), I remembered having imagined as a schoolgirl that I could *feel* a war going on in my head that kept me from making sense of the words on a page and that made the words I spoke come out differently from the way I had intended.

As my symptoms improved through the years, I was less and less troubled by this cerebral anarchy (did the two hemispheres slowly learn to cooperate instead of fighting for dominance?), but there has never been a time when I haven't had to compensate for my disorder. Although I have now published four books and numerous articles, my visual memory for the way a word looks is still so untrustworthy that my spelling, though better than it was even twenty years ago, is still a tiresome reminder of the old days. (An invaluable tool for me is Rudolf Flesch's little dictionary *Look It Up*. Flesch seems to know exactly which words I'm likely to be confused about.)

Early in my career as a writer, I learned to accept (though grudgingly) that I would have to make many more drafts than others to get what I wanted on the page. When my friends began using word processors and urged me to get one, I held back, convinced that I would have great difficulty learning to use it. And I did. At first I hated the machine, hated especially the (to me) unreadable manual. But once I learned how to use it, I began to enjoy the facility with which I could correct errors, and found that it saved me hours of retyping those endless drafts I used to have to make.

My memory for proper names and titles of books is no more dependable than it ever was, but as my contemporaries begin to suffer from memory loss for the first time and worry about the onset of Alzheimer's, I find I'm not much worse off than they are and there is no mystery about what ails me.

An area where I have made no progress is in orientation. I still come out of the subway and head north when I want to go south. In a car, when I'm given the job of navigating, and say, "Turn right," my husband smiles and says, "Are you sure it isn't left?" No, I'm not sure. In all likelihood it *is* left. And when I hear a friend say, casually, that she flew to such-and-such a place, rented a car at the airport, and found her destination in a strange city, I am in awe of such competence.

So my struggle continues. As I said at the end of *Reversals*, "Each new step [in my progress] is nothing more than a temporary resting place. A new dissatisfaction, coupled with a spurt of energy, will drive me on to yet another stage in the unending striving to be cured."

E.S.

Preface

There was something wrong with my brain. What had previously been a shadowy suspicion that hovered on the edge of consciousness became certain knowledge the year I was nine and entered fourth grade. I seemed to be like other children, but I was not like them: I could not learn to read or spell. Had my present friends, acquaintances, colleagues, and I grown up together, there would have been an abyss between them and me. The books they were then reading, I did not read. Their compositions merited gold stars, won prizes; mine were unacceptable. They were at the top of their classes; I was at the bottom. Throughout my childhood and youth the nature of my disorder remained mysterious to me and those in my milieu. When I was twenty-two it was diagnosed — not by a psychologist but by a poet: I was dyslexic.

Much later, when I had become sufficiently detached from the past to want to understand it, I discovered that what I had thought was a unique affliction occurs in all countries of the world, in all classes of society, and seems to have little to do with cultural, emotional, or family circumstances. Roughly one tenth of the population is dyslexic. There are those who believe that in the United States alone as many as 23 million are affected to some degree, as compared, say, with two million American stutterers.

Statesmen, public servants, generals, surgeons, writers — Woodrow Wilson, Nelson Rockefeller, General George Patton, Dr. Harvey Cushing, Gustave Flaubert, Hans Christian Andersen, and W. B. Yeats — are counted among their number.

Although the word *dyslexia* (often used loosely and inaccurately) has become fashionable today, a good deal about it remains obscure, and many of its victims continue to go unrecognized and untreated. Experts in the field have been hampered in their research because they have not been able to find out what it is like, from the inside, to live in a literate society and be unable to read and write. What has been wanting is the dyslexic's own story. As Dr. Lloyd J. Thompson has said in his book, *Reading Disabilities: Developmental Dyslexia:*

> Very few anonymous reports . . . of dyslexia can be found in the literature . . . The writer has attempted many times to persuade dyslexics to write their personal experiences, but without success. It is possible that these people are still sensitive about their handicap, or that they have glossed over, forgotten or repressed the details of the traumatic experiences. Or that they still have difficulty putting their experiences into correctly spelled words. For this reason they may be reluctant to reveal any vulnerable spot to a secretary available to do the writing for them.

The autobiographical accounts one does find are brief, and, for all the reasons suggested, anonymous or pseudonymous. Even nowadays, when the confessional mode is in style, and people talk candidly about what used to be called their private lives, the inhibition against revealing intellectual failures and limitations is strong. The old shame and fear of ridicule remain forever lively. Andersen was world famous and much decorated when he wrote:

Isn't it strange that·at the age of 66 I can still suffer and feel those torments of my youth . . . ? In my dreams I am still a schoolboy and Meisling [his teacher] is rude . . .

For years now I have "passed." Were it not for the periodic threats of exposure — anyone who passes learns to live with them — I would almost have forgotten what it was like to live in the limbo of illiteracy. But in order to write this book under my own name, I had to fight the old shame and the new fear of being patronized: I suffered a relapse. My symptoms returned full-blown, providing me with a sharp reminder of what life had been like before I was "cured." There are undoubtedly details of the early years that I have forgotten. Others that remain repressed. Everything that I remember I have set down, as I remember it.

Reversals

Chapter I

Having made a strenuous effort to understand the symbols he could make nothing of, he [Gustave Flaubert] wept giant tears . . .

For a long time he could not understand the elementary connection that made of two letters one syllable, of several syllables a word.

Souvenirs Intimes by Caroline
Commanville (Flaubert's niece)

The fall term was already under way when my sister and I were registered at P.S. 52, an elementary school in Inwood at the upper tip of Manhattan Island. At the principal's office we were separated. A messenger led me through a dank tunnel to one of the many annexes of the red-brick building. Constructed in 1857, it had served the community well until the recent influx of families, such as ours, who had left Chelsea and other older neighborhoods that were becoming increasingly commercial, families attracted by the greensward of natural playgrounds that surrounded Inwood valley and gave it a suburban air. The messenger led me up a flight of stairs, through a maze of corridors, and down a hall. She knocked on the door of a fourth grade classroom.

A geography lesson was in progress. An elderly spinsterish-looking woman, who had been holding a pointer to a map, took the note the messenger handed her. It was a brief account of my previous education: kindergarten through second grade at a boarding school run by nuns in Dobbs Ferry; third grade at a nonsectarian school in Farmingdale, New Jersey. While the teacher read it, I stood with my hands linked behind my back, eighty eyes focused on me. Slim and tall for my age, with copper-colored hair, I felt very much the new girl and wished I could take cover.

After assigning the class "busy work," the teacher motioned me to sit in a chair next to her desk. She handed me a paper covered with arithmetic problems and told me to go to work. Bewildered by my new surroundings, by the circuitous route I had traveled to $4A^2$, by the size of the class, and, above all, by the curtness of the instructions, I tried to make out what I was supposed to do. Was it a test? Addition, subtraction, and multiplication problems were jumbled together. Subtractions were easy to recognize; they were always just two stories high. Divisions were under those little shelters. What about the others? The sign in front of this one means (didn't it?) to multiply. Yet if it was multiplication, why were there so many numbers? It must be a problem meant for a higher grade. Perhaps a mistake had been made and I was being given a test meant for my sister. She was a year older and in fifth grade. Where was Marie? Always before in school she had been in the room next to mine. How would I find her at lunch time? It would be hours before then. Hours more before we could go home.

The teacher, whose hair was arranged like an inverted bird's nest, with twiggy-looking gray hairpins sticking out this way and that, said time was up. She frowned at my paper, slashing it with giant X marks made with a red pencil. Didn't I know my multiplication tables?

I wondered at her question. Of course I knew them. What must have happened was that I'd mixed up the signs and had added where I should have multiplied. The × and + signs had a way of spinning around — ×+ ×+ ×+×+×+ — faster and faster, like the spokes of a bicycle wheel, so that I couldn't tell one from another. Would I now be assigned a seat and be permitted to melt into the class?

The teacher handed me a book and, indicating the place, asked me to read.

At a glance I could see that this reader was harder than the one we'd used in Farmingdale. The print was smaller and there were more words on the page. I looked over the first sentence, trying to make out what it said.

"Aloud," the teacher barked.

Aloud? Bewilderment gave way to alarm. As I hadn't been asked to read aloud since second grade, I'd thought there would be no more oral reading. In Farmingdale the class had read in unison, or our teacher had asked for volunteers. It had never occurred to me to volunteer.

"Speak up! I haven't got all day."

The book, my hands holding it, the page looked as if I were staring down at them from a great height. The text became a gray blur, a screen on which I projected wavy lines.

By the chalky odor her clothes gave off, I could tell the teacher was leaning closer to me. I kept my eyes riveted to the page.

"What's this word?" She hit the first word with her pencil. I flinched as if she'd hit me.

"You don't know? What's this one? This one?"

I was not looking at the words. All my attention was concentrated on my throat and teeth. Swallowing hard and clamping my jaws together as tightly as I could, I had but one thought: I must not let a room full of strangers see me cry.

"Well, we'll see about *this!*" The teacher appointed a monitor to look after the class. She marched me down the hall, down the stairs, and through the tunnel to the main building. At the principal's office, she demanded to see Mr. Snyder. Was he trying to ruin her last year before retirement? Her class was already overcrowded. There was no room for another child, especially one who didn't belong in fourth grade. This one multiplied when she was supposed to add. And as for reading . . . it was a question whether she was at second-grade level.

Mr. Snyder knew Aunt Agnes. He knew also that she was assistant to the principal at P.S. 10 in Harlem. To placate the teacher — Miss Henderson he called her — he agreed to telephone Aunt Agnes. Could she explain the poor showing I'd made on the tests?

Aunt Agnes expressed surprise at what Mr. Snyder had to say. As we had just come to live with her she could only guess at what had happened. It was my first day in public school. I had never been in a class with more than ten children, so perhaps it was a question of shyness. It was also possible that the Farmingdale school, where we had been sent for our health, was not up to the standards of the New York City schools. In any case there was no question of my being made to repeat third grade. Only retarded children repeated in the lower grades. And, besides, I'd undoubtedly catch up quickly.

No, no question of my having to repeat, Mr. Snyder said, feeling the force of Aunt Agnes's personality through the receiver. The school could count on her to supervise my homework should it be required, could it not? That was probably all that would be necessary.

Miss Henderson was not reassured by this conversation. "All that would be necessary" indeed! Did Mr. Snyder expect her to produce miracles? On the march back to the classroom, she told me that she had a reputation as a teacher. She had never had a pupil leave her class without knowing how to read. *And she didn't intend to begin now!*

Miss Henderson lost no time in attacking what quickly became known as "the problem." The following day she called on me to take my turn during the oral reading lesson. The story, as I could make it out from the recitation of the others in my row, was about a man called Giant Whirligig. Or it was about the wind. Or both. I listened hard, trying to make sense of what I heard. When my turn came, I studied the black-and-white illustration that accompanied the text, searching for a clue. Buried in swirly black lines was the evil-looking face of a man, his cheeks puffed out. This must be Whirligig. The puffed cheeks . . . was it the story about blowing someone's house down?

Miss Henderson, who was pacing the front of the room, said, "I'm waiting."

The words, "I'm waiting," and the ring of irritability in

the voice, dislodged a memory. I was in the second grade classroom at Dobbs Ferry. It was early enough in the term for the windows to be open on a day of Indian summer, late enough for there to be a dunce — had it been Lina that day? — with a tall pointed hat standing in the corner of the room. I had been standing by the side of my desk for what seemed an eternity, a mustard-colored book, *Bible Stories for Children*, in my hand. The spine of my copy had sprung loose, exposing linen threads and blobs of glue, one of which I was worrying with my fingers. The room was quiet but for the sound of insects buzzing at the windows and the squeak of nun's shoes pacing the aisles. The class seemed to be holding its breath. Mother Cecilia broke the silence to remind me that she was "waai . . . ting."

Letting go of the glue, I made a fresh attempt to focus on the text. The initial letter of the story was bold and black. It went down steep and fast, ending in a hook, like the playground, slide. I traced it with my "reading finger" and prayed for a miracle. Tears came instead. One of them made a blot on the page which the coarse paper drank into the shape of an ill-drawn star. The words broke down into smeary letters, swam toward one another, and collided.

A voice nearby prompted. Far gone in terror, I heard only a roar in my head that sounded as if I were holding a conch shell to my ear. There was the swish of a ruler. Then WHACK: The prompter had caught it. The squeaky shoes came closer and closer. I waited, frozen, for the ear pull that would drag me to the dunce's corner. Instead the heavy hand that fell on my shoulder eased me down into my seat.

Tessa, called on in my place, covered my shame with her singsong voice. After I had stopped crying, and could listen again, I made out that it was the story about Jonah and the whale. How could the others tell what the words meant *just by looking?* And why, I wondered, my alarm increasing, had I escaped punishment? The crime of the current dunce was that she had read poorly, whereas I had not read at all. It must be that whatever was the matter with me — and surely it was something grave if all the others could make words out of the letters, and, even more remarkable, string the words together so that they told a story — it must be that whatever was the matter with me was beyond punishment. I searched for an explanation, and found one. Often when we had gone on outings to the nearby village, we had seen an ill-tempered dwarf who made rude and incomprehensible remarks as we passed by the bench where he sat. The nuns had taught us not to stare at him. We were to avert our eyes and say silently, "God bless the mark!" Mother Cecilia had averted her eyes. She must silently have said the prayer for me.

It may have seemed to her as the term progressed that He was not only blessing but helping me. If I was called on in the middle of a story, I read as well as or better than my classmates. My index finger moved across the page at the proper speed. I hesitated just the right amount of time between words. Memory (we read the stories over and over again) took me a long way. Actresslike, I studied to improve my performance. Over big words I pretended to stumble. From time to time, mimicking the other children, I appealed to the teacher for help on a word that was "too hard." Although I could as well have looked out the window, or at the blackboard, I had to remember to keep my eyes on the book. In order to know when to turn the page, I watched my neighbors covertly.

Called on to begin a story, I was at a loss, until I learned to associate the look of the page with the title. The first page of the Wedding Feast of Cana had a mole-like imperfection in the paper, say. Or the corner of the Jonah story was dog-eared. Or the beginning of the Loaves and Fishes hung loose from the binding. How was Mother Cecilia to understand what had gone wrong when, called on to begin a story whose first page offered no secret cue, I reverted to useless tracing of letters, and to tears? Each time it happened I waited in terror, waited and waited to be dragged to the dunce's corner. And each time Mother Cecilia averted her gaze. She spared me the humiliation of the pointed hat at the price of strengthening my suspicion: In a way more hidden and mysterious, there was something as wrong with me as there was with the dwarf.

At Farmingdale there had been no dwarf, and no oral reading. Health, not school work, was the important thing. The only tests we had to pass were medical ones (Had we gained weight? Did the X rays show our lungs were stronger?). The two hours we spent in class each day went by swiftly, our lessons frequently interrupted for breathing exercises and deep knee bends. During reading period I followed along with my finger while the volunteers read. When the class read in unison, I chanted as loudly and as happily as the others. My failures in Mother Cecilia's class faded from memory. And before long I had the illusion that I read as well as my classmates.

So what apprehension I had felt the first morning I'd set off for public school had had to do not with school work but with being a new girl in strange surroundings. If the placement tests had set off an alarm bell, it was only now, having to read aloud before the class, that I remembered the Dobbs Ferry dwarf. It was his face I superimposed on the face of Giant Whirligig.

"Has the cat got your tongue?" Miss Henderson asked. "Come up here. Come up and face the class."

My legs seemed to be beyond my control.

Miss Henderson advanced on me and pulled me to the front of the room. "Now: *Read.*"

What I had dreaded in Mother Cecilia's class, and had imagined I'd escape, had been lurking in my future. Even wearing the dunce cap would have been less mortifying than my present state. The dunce faced the wall, whereas I was made to face forty children, naked, the only cover for my shame a blush that felt like liquid fire.

A voice said, "Crying's not going to get you anywhere."

The voice said a great many other things. I didn't hear them. Blocking my ears, I kept repeating to myself, "This isn't me. I'm not here. This isn't me. I'm not here." When, finally, I was allowed to return to my seat, I put my head on the desk, folded my arms over it, and wept bitter tears.

That my mutism infuriated Miss Henderson I understood very soon. In the days that followed it became clear that she felt it was something I was doing to her. It made her feel powerless, out-of-control. She didn't know how to cope with it. "Speak up! *Speak Up!*" she'd shout, giving up all pretense of controlling her temper. "If you persist in being stubborn . . . ," or "If you persist in being mulish . . . ," or "If you continue to defy me, you'll get a failure in conduct as well as in reading."

Stubborn? Mulish? These accusations surprised and wounded me. Even-tempered and submissive by nature, being good had always come easily to me. The exigent nuns at Dobbs Ferry had considered me a model of good conduct. It had made me a school favorite. The threat of a double failure, together with the habit of wishing to please, forced me to "speak up," although I knew it would get me into deeper trouble. The words I knew, I said. Others I guessed at. A letter here, a configuration there gave me a clue. Sometimes I guessed right ("Whirligig," for example, was easy to spot. It didn't look like anything else). More often, of course, I guessed wrong. Whereupon Miss Henderson would shout, "Wrong! Wrong!" Then with a "Class?" she'd invite my classmates to correct me. They did so with gusto. Their roar often frightened me (for by now I was so jumpy everything frightened me) so that I didn't catch what they said. Which meant that if the word was repeated in the next sentence, I would be stuck again. What could I do then but be silent?

Mutism, temper, humiliation, tears. Mutism, temper, humiliation, tears. So went the inescapable and inexorable round of my days.

My nights were troubled by dreams in which Miss Henderson, Whirligig, and the mocking chorus figured prominently. I awakened feeling dull and achy, as if I were coming down with the flu. I ate breakfast without appetite, dragged myself to school, and waited through the other lessons in a state of apprehension for the oral reading period. Afterward, red-eyed, sore, and spent, I waited to be released by the three o'clock bell.

Arnie Rothstein alone made life supportable. Arnie was the smartest student in the class, as one could tell by his homework notebook, which was a firmament of glittering gold and silver stars. Aside from intelligence, he also had long curly eyelashes and a scout knife which he wore, with what seemed to me incredible daring, in the outside pocket of his laced-to-the-knee boots. Having overheard at home an adult conversation about Arnold Rothstein, a gangster whose career and electrocution were periodically rehashed in the pages of the rotogravure (where he was called "the J. P. Morgan of the Underworld"), I imagined, mistakenly, that Arnie was his son. How else explain Arnie's devil-may-care attitude? In his fearless way, he took terrible chances for me. He corrected my arithmetic homework in the school yard before we filed into class. He showed me his paper during spelling tests. In oral reading it was Arnie's prompting more often than my guessing that helped me to get a word right here and there. When I was made to go to the front of the room, he could do nothing for me. After I had stumbled back to my seat and had wept my heart out, I would find him looking at me, his eyes brimming over with compassion. The look in those dark eyes was like a magic balm. It eased my pain, made me feel less freakish. I was not an outcast. No matter how badly I performed, there was one person in the room who was on my side. Criminal's son or not, I fell head over heels in love with Arnie Rothstein.

Since I had said nothing at home about my daily agony in 4A², my first month's report card came as a disagreeable surprise. Not having heard from Mr. Snyder or from my teacher again, Aunt Agnes had taken it that, my shyness overcome, I was now catching up to the public school level. Of my earlier academic difficulties, she had had no inkling. The transfer from the Dobbs Ferry School had not mentioned my erratic performance in oral reading. From Farmingdale there had been only the comment that I had satisfactorily completed the work of third grade.

Miss Henderson's report was blunt: "Failure" in reading. There was an asterisk after this grade directing the eye to a covering letter in which Miss Henderson threatened that if I did not practice reading aloud at home every evening and show *marked* improvement, there was not the slightest chance that I would be promoted at the end of the year to fifth grade.

Aunt Agnes had recently asked us to call her Auntie, to mark her role as guardian and distinguish her from our other aunts (for although we had neither parent, our mother having died when I was two months old and our father when I was five, we had a large family — a maternal grandmother, a host of aunts, uncles, great aunts and great uncles, cousins and cousins-once-removed). It was as guardian that she studied the report card, looked from it to the letter and back again in perplexity and disbelief. She took off her spectacles, which pinched the flesh of her nose, and put them into a little black box with a lid that snapped shut. Without her glasses she looked, with her high wide brow and Roman nose, like Christopher Columbus, or at least the bust of him that was in the school auditorium. Her white hair, rinsed blue by an overzealous hairdresser, was set in deep blue waves through which I sometimes imagined the *Niña*, the *Pinta*, and the *Santa Maria* sailing.

Auntie congratulated Marie on her string of A's, signed her card, and dismissed her. She took up my card again and held it against her lips. She blew a hissing noise against its edge. This meant that she was dangerously vexed but uncertain what course of action to take. "Tsssssss."

It made the sound of steam about to blow the lid off a pot.

"Tsssssss." She waved the card at me. "What is the meaning of this?"

What could I say? When she pressed me, I offered the excuse that Miss Henderson's reader was "too hard."

Auntie took out her glasses and pinched them onto her nose again. "Bring it to me."

Miss Henderson's power over me was not in her tongue, though I shrank from its lashes, but in the way she used my classmates as spectators at the side show in which I was the freak. Auntie needed no outside assistance. In her person and in her manner, she was Authority. The command to bring my book to her was the moment of truth.

On the way to my room I flirted with saying I'd left my reader in school. But Auntie would find another book, one that might be even harder.

"Let me hear the lesson you've prepared for tomorrow," she said when I stood before her, my reader in hand.

With no idea how to prepare a lesson, I had this evening, as every other evening, sat looking at the book with unfocused eyes. It would not do to say this, I knew. Instead I read the lesson we had been over in class that day. Ordinarily memory would have taken me a certain way, but in Miss Henderson's class I was so apprehensive waiting for my turn to come, and so miserable after it, that I wasn't able to listen while the others read. Reading to Auntie I found that my memory of the day's lesson ran out after the first few words.

"Continue," Auntie urged.

Clearly she was not going to prompt me or help me sound out the next word. She expected me to read until I reached a natural stopping place. So I read. That is to say I repeated my daily performance. I clutched at recognizable words, guessed at others, and invented what I thought would make a suitable connective. As I went along, and Auntie made no corrections, my spirits lifted. I had the impression that I *was* reading, just as I had had when I'd recited from memory at Dobbs Ferry, or had followed the lead of the class at Farmingdale.

A clap of thunder brought my improvisation to an end. *"What is this gibberish?* I can't believe my ears. *Do you hear what you're saying?"*

I didn't say so, but no, I didn't hear. I never heard what I was saying when I read. I was too busy translating what I saw on the page into what I thought everyone else saw.

"Anyone would think you were holding the book *upside down."* Auntie grabbed the book from my hand. No, I had been holding it properly. Ominously echoing Miss Henderson she asked, "What's this word?"

Now that the bubble had burst, and I understood that whatever I had been doing it could not be called reading, I knew I had no chance of success if I tried to say what a word was.

"What's this word?" Auntie pointed to another. *"How is it possible? You seem to know nothing. Do you even know the alphabet?"*

Auntie sounded scared. The terror in her voice frightened me more than anything previously had done.

"Stop crying. Now listen to me. And listen carefully. From

now on you're to bring me your book every evening after dinner, do you hear?" As Auntie signed my report card, she added, "I'm going to write a note for you to take to Miss Henderson. I'll tell her that *I* will see to it that you learn to read. *And no nonsense about it.*"

Chapter II

My father was an angry and impatient teacher and flung the reading book at my head . . .

Autobiographies, by W. B. Yeats

I remember vividly the pain and mortification I felt as a boy of 8, when I was assigned to read a short passage of Scripture at a community vesper service during summer vacation in Maine — and did a thoroughly miserable job of it.

Nelson Rockefeller, in *TV Guide*, October 16, 1976

Three o'clock, when school was dismissed, was no longer a moment of liberation. After Auntie took over the role of teacher, going home was as much to be dreaded as going to school. Following a brief play period, I went to my room to prepare for the evening lesson. Or, since I had no idea how to prepare, what I did was worry. And as I worried, a going-to-the-doctor feeling grabbed hold of me, squeezing my heart and my stomach. I ate dinner listlessly. As soon as I could, I excused myself and went to my room, hoping to be forgotten. The command to appear before Auntie was not long in coming.

"The sooner we get to the lesson, the sooner it will be over" was Auntie's usual opening remark.

Reluctant to make the first mistake, I delayed as long as possible. I had difficulty finding the place. I had forgotten my handkerchief (which I was sure to have need of), and had to go back to my room to get it.

"Why are you stalling? You seem determined to try my patience."

Miss Henderson and now Auntie: There seemed to be nothing I could do to please either of them. How, in the past, had it been so easy, so effortless to be a favorite? With a feeling of impending doom I would begin. I might get halfway through the first sentence before Auntie would say in a dry, controlled voice, "In the context the word cannot possibly be 'saw.' 'The man saw going home.' Does that make sense to you? It must be 'was.'"

I'd repeat, "The man was going home." In the next sentence, or the one after, meeting the word again, I'd hesitate.

Had I said 'was' before and had Auntie corrected it to 'saw,' or vice versa? My brain ached.

"Don't tell me you don't recognize that word. *I just told it to you.* You're *not trying.*"

Both my teachers accused me of not trying. They had no idea what an effort I was making. Was, saw, was, saw. How were they so sure which it was? Rattled by Auntie's foot tapping, I decided for "saw."

"No, no, NO. How *can* you be so stupid? The word is 'was.' WASWASWAS. And for heaven's sake *stop sniveling.* If those nuns hadn't fallen for your tears, you'd be able to read by now and we wouldn't be going through this . . ."

The burden of teaching, which Auntie had avoided in her career, preferring administrative work, made her so irascible that every evening there was a crisis. The all-too-brief interval between dinner and bedtime, during which she and Aunt Lucy (her younger sister who lived with us) had formerly read the newspaper while Marie and I had listened to the radio, had become the most painful period of the day. Aunt Lucy and Marie, unwilling auditors, hid behind closed doors and blocked their ears, struggling with resentment, one evening against Auntie for losing her temper, another evening against me for provoking her with my stupidity. It was hard to be sympathetic for long with anyone who missed easy words even a moron would know.

Aunt Lucy tried to tell Auntie what Auntie already knew but wouldn't admit, that the pedagogical role didn't suit her; she should give it up. Hadn't she noticed that I was getting worse instead of better? When I'd come to them from Farmingdale I had seemed as lively and bright as any nine-year-old. Now I behaved as though I were dull-witted. The expression on my face, even my posture, had changed. How was it that someone who was good at sports and danced well could now be so physically awkward, always tripping over her own feet, falling so often her knees were chronically scraped? And what were those crazy words I made up which so patently had nothing to do with what was on the page and sounded like pidgin English? To say nothing of the baby talk — "ninimun" for "minimum," "buff cuttons" for "cuff buttons."

Auntie said she had no intention of giving up the lessons. If she didn't take the responsibility for teaching me to read, who would?

The lessons continued, Auntie grimly determined, I increasingly despairing. She shouted, I cried, the others hid. The night I read "off" for "of" for the third time (as in, "He was off the same family as the old man"), Auntie exploded. She flew out of the chair, grabbed the book from my hand, and hurled it at my head. When it hit me, we were both astonished and shaken.

The following evening Auntie came to the lesson with a fresh resolve. She made a "saintly effort" to correct and repeat with no rise in inflection. By the time she dismissed me she looked pale and drawn, as do athletes who have overextended themselves. The strain was so great she couldn't keep it up. As time went on the lessons had less and less to do with reading. They became skirmishes in a war of nerves, each side, knowing how dangerous an engagement could be, straining for control — Auntie with her temper, I with my "idiotic errors" and ungovernable tears.

Before each lesson I told myself to go slowly. Slowly, slowly. I tried to make my eyes move in an orderly way along the line. By sub-vocalization, I studied to get the words right before pronouncing them aloud. Above all, I admonished myself to keep calm, to fight the panic, opaque as fog, numbing as ether, which rolled in and settled on my brain.

In an effort to be more tolerant with me, Auntie began to look for a scapegoat. Miss Henderson's reader was at fault.

Why was she using an old-fashioned text full of murky allegories about nature when the other fourth grade classes used a modern reader with stories more likely to interest nine-year-olds? In her elegant Palmer Method handwriting, Auntie wrote Miss Henderson. (The two teachers, who sometimes cooperated, sometimes competed, carried on a spirited correspondence, with me as letter carrier.) By return mail, Miss Henderson, whose penmanship was if anything more elegant than Auntie's, replied that she had been using the Whirligig book with great success for forty years and saw no reason to change on the eve of her retirement: It was the child who was at fault, not the book.

What, Auntie wanted to know, had my third grade teacher at Farmingdale been up to? Had that Miss Barnes taught me *nothing* all year?

While I rejoiced to hear Miss Henderson attacked, I was defensive of Miss Barnes. How I longed for those happy days of mindless chanting, the choral lessons in Miss Barnes's class. I looked back on them as an overburdened woman looks back on a carefree childhood.

By third grade even a slow child would have felt a strong desire to read — storybooks, the comics, letters from home. Had I never looked at a page of words, Auntie said, and said to myself, "I want to know what these words mean"?

The question confused me. On the one hand I had had the impression in third grade that I *was* reading in class. On the other, there was a memory that didn't jibe with this impression. On St. Valentine's day Miss Barnes had given us crayon and paper, paste-pot and brush to make valentines with. By dinner time, when the cards were to be delivered, the excitement between the sexes (new to one who had previously been in an all girls' school) had reached fever pitch. The girls, mindful of snoopers, read their messages furtively, then looked smug or conspiratorial. The boys, reading theirs, broke into maniacal laughter.

The large envelope placed in my hand contained a white lace heart which had been pasted onto a folded sheet of red paper. Inside stood a boy, one hand on his heart, the other extended in a beseeching gesture. He was reciting a poem, as the comic strip balloon which came out of his mouth showed. What did it say? Without the chorus behind me, I found I couldn't make out the words. And I wanted to desperately. For this was not any old story like *Hans Brinker,* or the comic strips, which didn't interest me. This was a message addressed to me. I recognized some of the words — "you," "be," "my." Not enough to tell me what the poem was about. Perhaps if I concentrated very hard, as Mother Cecilia used to urge us to do, the message would come to me. Concentrating, as usual, didn't help. The picture gave me a clue. The boy was asking for something. *What could it be?* Reluctantly I slipped the card back into the envelope and assumed what I hoped was a knowing expression, in case anyone at my table was looking at me. At bedtime, when Marie and I had a moment alone, I asked her to read it to me. (She always read me the letters from home, so she didn't find this an unusual request.) As it was the first poem addressed to me, and afterward I "read" it to myself many times, I remember it exactly.

> Do you?
> Don't you?
> Will you?
> Won't you?
> BE MY VALENTINE?

it pleaded. In the place where a signature should have been there was a large question mark made with India ink. Jimmy was the only one in the class who had used India ink. If the syntax of the poem was tenuous, the message was clear. Cupid's arrow made its first strike at my heart: aetat eight and a half.

Since I could no more tell Auntie about Jimmy and the valentine than I could have told her about my secret crush on Arnie, I simplified and said no, I had never felt a desire to read.

If that was the case, the nuns were to blame. They must have stifled my natural interest in reading in the lower grade. Auntie, who had a strong anticlerical streak, had never approved of the way the nuns did things. If Miss Henderson's methods were old-fashioned, the nuns' methods were medieval. Hadn't they — she became indignant all over again thinking about it — hadn't they changed my writing hand without asking my father's permission?

The summer before I entered first grade, I had looked forward impatiently to learning to write. At "The Hedges," a Victorian seaside hotel on Long Island where my father's family moved for the summer, I spent rainy days covering pages of scrap paper with arabesques I liked to think looked like letters. I would look at the marks I'd made and say to myself with a thrill of excitement, "I'm writing!" When formal lessons in penmanship began in first grade, the preference I showed for using my left hand, which heretofore no one had commented on, distressed the first grade teacher. It was as if Mother Serafina had discovered in me a moral flaw. Each time she caught me with the pencil in my "bad" hand, she put it into the "good" one. I would have made the change to please her had I not been delighted with my left-handed skill in making letters and dismayed at my right-handed squiggles. And the right way *felt* so wrong that the pencil had a way of returning to where it more comfortably rested. If I heard the teacher approaching and realized the pencil was in my left hand, I quickly transferred it. The reward for switching was a contemptuous comment, "Chicken scratch," when she picked up my paper and examined it.

A showdown came the day we were to display our newly acquired skill by writing a letter home. The brief message was written on the blackboard. We had only to copy it. The other children made practice trials in pencil and then were given writing paper and ink. The lesson was over and I was still laboring on yellow paper. After class was dismissed for the day, I was kept in. If it took all afternoon, my teacher said, she would keep me at my desk until I wrote properly. When the bell rang for supper, in desperation she gave me ink and stationery. On the first piece of paper I pressed down so awkwardly I made a hole. On the second, I made a shameful blot. In the end, with me in tears and Mother Serafina beside herself with vexation, she cupped her hand around mine and guided it over the letters.

On those rainy days at "The Hedges" when I had played at writing, I had not imagined that it would be so disagreeable to be taught the real thing. My right hand felt trapped, imprisoned in the larger, more powerful hand. I relaxed my grip on the pen, let my fingers go limp. It was Mother Serafina who wrote the letter home, not I. But the possessor of the stronger hand also possessed the stronger will. By the end of the term I was as right-handed as all the other children. Or so it seemed.

My father had been displeased when he discovered the forced change. Auntie, who knew the practice had been abandoned some years earlier in the public schools, had been concerned that it might have done me some harm, especially as she'd noticed that I'd remained, in other ways, strongly left-sided — sighting with my left eye, listening on the phone with my left ear. Wasn't it possible, she asked now, that the change was in some way responsible for my inability to learn to read? And wouldn't you think that having been so strict about writing, the nuns would have been equally demanding about the far more important subject of reading? Marie had received excellent instruction. How was it I had been permitted to fake my way through second grade? Marie, when questioned, said that it was because I was the school favorite.

Except for the letter-writing incident, I was never punished (whereas Marie, who was as rebellious as she was bright, frequently had been).

Sickly, docile, and devout: Yes, Auntie could imagine that these qualities would have made me a favorite. It was probably my physical frailty, however, that explained Mother Cecilia's willingness to ignore my inability to read. She must have decided that a child who had received extreme unction three times was not likely to live long. One winter the fever that accompanied my annual bout of pneumonia would go so high the doctor would not be able to bring it down. Therefore, I should be prepared for death, not life. I was taught a catechism well above my grade level (which I learned without difficulty), and by special dispensation I was confirmed at age six, it being thought that I probably wouldn't survive to the statutory age of eight. To the nuns' way of thinking, Auntie said with a sardonic laugh, a left-handed child would be offensive to the Almighty, an illiterate one would not.

To find a scapegoat was only momentarily gratifying. The problem remained and had to be dealt with. Auntie, who thought of herself as an amateur psychologist, made an effort to "understand" me as she tried to understand disruptive children at P.S. 10. When she wasn't angry at me, she did not believe I was mentally deficient. Illnesses apart, I had developed normally: had been trained, had walked and talked at the proper times, had got on well with other children. What, then, was the matter?

My maternal grandmother, when she heard Auntie's concern, answered unhesitatingly that there was nothing the matter with me. Why all this fuss about reading? Was Auntie trying to make a bluestocking out of me? I'd read when I was ready. Grandmother's certainty I found comforting but surprising. How could she be so sure? Did she know something Auntie didn't know? (She did, as I later discovered.)

Miss Henderson had no patience with my grandmother's indulgent attitude, and thought psychology was a euphemism for mollycoddling. She was clear in her mind that the problem was less the result of stupidity, although she thought I was certainly at best borderline, than of laziness and carelessness. It was no good my knowing that 6 × 6 equals 36 if on the exam I wrote 63. My right-handed penmanship, while far from pretty, was acceptable, but again I couldn't seem to copy anything from the blackboard the way it was written. My memory was of the "Swiss-cheese variety" — strong in some areas, nonexistent in others. Where it was nonexistent, it was the result of inattentiveness. It was inattentiveness that made my spelling "completely unacceptable." In her initial alarm about my reading, Miss Henderson had overlooked my poor spelling. Now my report cards carried another "Failure."

While I have no record of how I read at that time, I do have a sample of my spelling. It is a letter written the previous year from Farmingdale. Since my spelling didn't improve for a long time, it gives an indication of the work I was handing in to Miss Henderson. Ordinarily I left it to Marie to correspond with our relatives, claiming that I never could think of "anything to say," so this letter was undoubtedly written as a class exercise. There are signs that Miss Barnes gave me considerable help with it. She probably also made suggestions about its contents. It reads:

Deare Uncel
The Dr. was hear today and examimimed us we are booth feeling well. I hope to hear from you soon the mail cames hear twiceaday. It is very nirl hear.we eat well and sleep well

Your loving nice.

This naked plea for mail — originally spelled "male," erased and corrected — was considerably worked over before it was sent out. The writing is legible (although with a strong downward slant to the right-hand corner), but the paper looks messy because of the large number of erasures. Even "The" was erased and rewritten. "Dr." must have been copied from the blackboard because I knew as little about abbreviations as I knew about punctuation. "Very" was begun as "yer"; "nirl" for "nice" may have been an example of the kind of fudging I practiced for years: When in doubt I wrote letters loosely, hoping the reader would credit me with the correct spelling.

Since Miss Henderson didn't permit erasures on test papers, and the only help I received — and that furtively — was from Arnie, it is small wonder that my spelling grade in 4A² was "Failure."

The day Miss Henderson observed that I skipped whole lines as well as words when I read, she sent me home with a note suggesting that my vision be checked. Auntie and I set off for the optometrist's office in high spirits, hoping for a cure. I longed for eyeglasses. Even if they didn't help me to read better, I would look so studious wearing them that Auntie and Miss Henderson would be convinced I was "trying." The optometrist dashed our hopes: vision — 20/20.

Weeks later there was another holiday. It occurred to Auntie that it was my hearing that was at fault. Why had she not thought of it immediately? As a child I had been troubled with earaches. The year I was in kindergarten my annual respiratory infection traveled to my ears. I held my head and whimpered. The day I lay down on the kindergarten floor and complained that my head was going to burst, the doctor was called. He wrapped me in a sheet, mummylike, and incised the eardrum. My temperature rose. My father, who had been summoned, was displeased with the way things were going. He hurried me from Dobbs Ferry to New York in an ambulance for a consultation with a specialist. After the examination, Dr. Gormley looked grave. He would have to perform a radical mastoidectomy on the right ear immediately. When I had recuperated, he would operate on the left ear, which was also infected. There was a very good chance, he warned, that I would be deaf.

At first my recovery was said to be miraculous. The left ear would not have to be operated on after all. The incision behind the right one was healing nicely. And, most astonishing of all, I had suffered no hearing loss.

Clearly I wasn't completely deaf. But perhaps there had been just sufficient hearing loss to explain why I would be told a word ten times and the following evening get it wrong again. Hopes high again, we set off to see an otologist. No luck with him either: My hearing was excellent.

There followed a longish, muted period during which Auntie was neither angry nor making an effort to control herself. She seemed patient in a new, preoccupied way. One night, overhearing the grownups talk, I understood why. Dr. Gormley again. Hadn't he told my father that he'd had to cut into my skull during the surgery? A slip of the chisel was all that would have been needed . . .

Had my brain been damaged? If further evidence was needed to confirm Auntie's suspicion, she had it the day she sent me on an errand to a new grocery store four blocks from home. I was so long in returning she demanded an explanation: Where had I been?

I had been lost.

Lost? How could I have been when the store was on Academy Street, the street we lived on? Was I sure I hadn't met a friend and dallied to play?

What had happened, as I tried to explain — not very clearly because I didn't understand it myself — was that coming out of the store I turned left instead of right. I walked four blocks in the wrong direction, saw that it was wrong, returned to the store, set out in the proper direction, looked for our building, number 341, in a row of identical apartment houses. Not finding it, I returned to the store, tried the other direction again. Back and forth I went, becoming more and more confused, then panicky. It seemed impossible that I could be so close to home and yet not be able to find my way. I saw it as another sign of my stupidity. By chance Ginny, the high school girl who lived in the apartment above ours, came along. I asked, as casually as I could, if she was going home and joined her. She talked animatedly about the prom they were preparing for at high school. Ordinarily I would have been greedy for the details. I thought high school an exciting place to be, because of Ginny's accounts of what went on there, and thought Ginny's life unimaginably glamorous. Instead of listening this time, I tried to think how I would explain my long absence to Auntie.

When we reached the house, I saw that I had passed it repeatedly in my search. I knew the number well enough, but had looked for 431 instead of 341. My incoherent explanation troubled rather than angered Auntie, especially as it reminded her that Miss Henderson had reported more than once that if I was sent on an errand to the main building at P.S. 52, I invariably lost my way back to the annex. Was a nine-year-old girl who had no sense of direction "all there"?

The old family doctor, the one my father had consulted whenever there had been a medical crisis at Dobbs Ferry, still practiced in Chelsea, around the corner from what had been my grandfather's house. Auntie decided to take me to see him. Dr. Hess knew my history and had Dr. Gormley's report of the ear surgery. The doctor received us in his parlor-floor consultation room. He flashed a bright light into my eyes, looked into my ears, hit my knees with a hammer, scraped down the sole of my feet with a metal instrument. He listened to my lungs, ran his fingers down my spine, weighed me. I had lost some of the weight I had gained at Farmingdale and showed signs of developing a slight cur-

vature of the spine that should be watched. Otherwise I was
fine. What was the problem?

Auntie gave him an expurgated version of what had been
happening in the past few months — my failure in school,
her attempts to teach me. Could the mastoidectomy . . . ?
Was there something the matter with the b–r–a–i–n? She
spelled the word, thinking I was as poor at guessing as I was
at spelling.

Dr. Hess made light of her concern. What impressed him
was how well I was doing, not how poorly. Was she forgetting what a sickly child I'd been? More than once he'd
thought I was a goner. Why worry about a little trouble in
school? I'd outgrow it, probably. A slow-developer. Maybe
even a nonreader. That was all. Not surprising when you
remembered the sky-high fevers and . . .

On the long subway ride home Auntie whistled her dry
whistle. Tsssssssss. At P.S. 10, her school, "slow-developer"
was a euphemism for retardation. There were special classes,
"ungraded" classes, for such children. She was angry with
Dr. Hess for suggesting that I was one of them (even though
the thought had crossed her mind more than once) and was
irritated with him for speaking as he had in front of me. It
was all very well for him to talk about patience, she said
aloud, but if I didn't learn to read now, it would ruin my
whole life. Before I knew it, I'd be put in a special class. If I
got into high school, which seemed unlikely at the rate I was
going, I would be "shunted" into the commercial course.

Nothing Auntie had previously threatened, and she threatened everything she could think of, had so chilled my blood.
My high school days ruined, too? The glimpses I had had of
George Washington High School, Ginny's high school, the
splendid edifice on top of Fort George whose gleaming cupola I looked up at from Inwood, had stimulated fantasies of
happier days to come. Elementary school, with its emphasis

on reading, spelling, and arithmetic, was a dreary stretch to be struggled through so that one would be free to go to high school. Ginny had assured me that Latin and geometry were not only more interesting but easier than subjects we studied at P.S. 52. Dreaming of an escape from the miseries of childhood and elementary school, I had seen myself, like her, wearing high-heeled shoes and a black crew-neck sweater with a giant orange W on it. Like her, I would be on the basketball team, and after school, I would walk down the hill, a boy at each elbow, talking excitedly about the coming prom. The gymnasium would be transformed with balloons and crepe paper into an ocean liner. The band would play "Avalon." In a white evening gown, I would glide around the floor in Arnie's arms, while those on the stag line waited impatiently to cut in. High school, a delightful way station on the express train to adulthood, was now endangered by my inability to read. I might not get there at all. Or if I did, I'd have to take the commercial course. I didn't know what that was, but it sounded punitive, a threat to my dreams.

Dr. Hess had unwittingly given Auntie a tonic. That evening she took up the lessons again with renewed vigor. Before beginning she made me a little speech. Children in ungraded classes were unfortunates who came from poor backgrounds and had inherited their defects. I came from a family of educators. Of *readers*. My paternal grandfather, who had been appointed by Mayor Grace as an honorary member of the New York City Board of Education, had taught his children to read. They had all learned *before* going to school. She, as I knew, was an omnivorous reader. So, too, had my father been. What would *he* have thought of my report cards?

I often wondered. When I should have been preparing my lesson, I found myself daydreaming about what life would have been like had my father, my indulgent father, not died when he was only thirty. He would not have scolded me, nor said I was stupid. He would have known what was wrong with me. Or, if he hadn't, he would have found a doctor to cure me, the way he had done when I had had those terrible earaches.

After a visit to my maternal grandmother, or to the great aunt and uncle with whom Marie and I spent Christmas and Easter vacations, I daydreamed that my father had named one of them guardian in his will. Grandmother, a tall, elegant woman who wore pearl earrings, a chin veil, and furs over her arms, thought girls should be dressed prettily and prepared for marriage. What was Auntie making all the fuss about? What was the hurry about my learning to read? I'd learn sooner or later.

Great uncle Charlie, who exaggerated my talent for music, thought I should be given a musical education. It was a source of astonishment to me, and a great comfort, that my mother's side of the family refused to believe anything was wrong with my brain. I say that it was comforting, but it was so only when I was with them. Back at school, or at home again, the evidence was too strong that there *was* something wrong. Still, it was a lifeline that I grabbed hold of when I thought I was drowning. And day-to-day it furnished material for daydreams: Wearing a blue velvet party dress Grandmother had bought me, I was singing "Drink to me only with thine eyes" to an admiring circle of relatives (who didn't know I couldn't read the words but had memorized them), while Uncle Charlie, glowing with pride, accompanied me at the piano.

"If you spent less time daydreaming and more time concentrating on your book," Auntie would say, catching me at it, "you'd be able to read by now."

If Auntie was tempted to abandon the lessons, my midterm report card, which carried renewed threats, spurred her on. She drove herself, and me, harder than ever: I would not be, could not be, left back.

How could I not be, I wondered, when every day even I had evidence that I didn't belong in fourth, much less fifth grade. When we were asked to fold our papers down from the top, I folded mine up from the bottom. (No, Arnie's eyes signaled: this way.) Asked to raise my right hand, I raised my left. Even assembly, one of the periods in the day I enjoyed because of the singing and marching, would have been spoiled if I'd listened to the left/right directions instead of going toward the piano (left), or toward the windows (right). Except for the gym class, which I also enjoyed and where in games we played I was surprisingly well-coordinated, my body seemed out of control. The curvature in my spine, which Dr. Hess had noted, became more obvious as my back seemed too heavy a burden for me to hold up. I was always tired. My legs buckled under me. I fell constantly, ripping my stockings and scraping my knees. I walked into objects as if they weren't there. The cord I pulled to turn on a light came off in my hand. When I prepared vegetables, I cut my finger. When I dried dishes, the breakage was high. I lost school books, lunch box, mittens, hats, and once, in the dead of winter, my coat.

Evening lessons were now a matter of routine despair. Having tried harder than ever when I heard my high school days were in jeopardy, without the least sign of success, I felt overwhelmed with impotence. The massive boulder under which I was pinned would not budge. I gave up struggling.

"You're not trying," Auntie shouted, terrified by my slackness. *"I'm doing this for your own good. Can't you understand?"*

Sometimes I tried to understand. I put myself in Auntie's place. This woman was not my mother. She didn't have to struggle to teach me to read. She could allow me to be put in the ungraded class. Why should she care? I imagined what it was like for her to come home from a bad day at school (a knife fight in the lunchroom, say, police, ambulances, a student rushed to the hospital, a hysterical mother to be calmed down: everyday occurrences at P.S. 10). Wearily, she called me for the lesson. I began to read in the usual halting, bumbling, maddening way. Her fatigue, frustration, concern about my future became almost palpable to me. In sympathy with her, I made up a new fantasy. I pictured, as vividly as I could, the strain of her work day, the reluctance with which she began the lesson. The reading went as usual until, because I tried extra, extra hard, it happened! The words began to spill out of my mouth as if Auntie herself were reading. My recitation was letter-perfect, I read "with expression" and, the ultimate test, with comprehension. So went the fantasy.

Empathy proved a dangerous strain. If I was on Auntie's side, I must be against mine. My low view of myself would drop lower. I would have to agree with Auntie that I was lazy and had a "loose moral fiber." But Auntie after all was Auntie and I, however gelatinously, was I. If I didn't hold tight to what there was of me, I might turn to liquid, like my tears, and evaporate.

Aunt Lucy suggested that I be tutored by Marie. Auntie wouldn't hear of it. That would increase my already excessive dependence on Marie. But wait . . . how about cousin Tom? My junior by six months, he would sharply point up my backwardness, and might even engender a spirit of competition.

This further indignity I had to tolerate only briefly. Tom's method was to mimic Auntie's. After he'd run through her catalogue of reproaches and invectives and couldn't think what next to do, we sat, he and I, in sticky silence. Discovering that to be a jailer can be almost as tedious and disagreeable as to be a prisoner, he soon asked to be released.

If during that year it occurred to me to be defiant, to shout back, to refuse to do the lesson, to storm out of the house, I must quickly have rejected the idea. Rebelliousness was the prerogative of bright children, I thought, like my sister.

Nor did I permit myself to give a name to the feelings of anger and rage I felt toward Auntie and Miss Henderson. To hate a human being, I had been taught, was a mortal sin. Fortunately the commandments left me a way out. They said nothing about hating objects. So I was free to hate books as much as I liked. And I hated them mightily. They were as repellent as snakes. And as disagreeable to handle. I avoided touching them whenever possible.

"Where is your reader?" Auntie would say, when she came home in the late afternoon and found me staring off into space. With a gesture of helplessness, I'd said I couldn't find it. An hour or so later, after the apartment had been combed and the reader found, I'd hear her complain to Aunt Lucy: "Can you believe it? This time I found it in the broom closet. Isn't she the *limit?* When she doesn't drop it, she misplaces or hides it. Do you think she does it on purpose?" To me she'd say, "Why did you hide it?"

"I didn't hide it," I'd claim, astonished that she imagined me capable of an action so spunky. "It just got there."

Lacking the courage for open rebellion, I turned to petty delinquency. Nothing had convinced me that the candy we had at home, which came in boxes and was doled out for good behavior, could compare with the penny candy the other children bought after school. If I ate a dry lunch, I could use the nickel Auntie gave me to buy milk with for penny candy. Old Mr. Samuelson, who owned the candy store, waited patiently behind the display case while my classmates and I agonized over our choices. There were green leaves, chicken feet, ropes of licorice, peppermint sticks, Mary Janes, bubble gum and the superior and more expensive double bubble gum, Tootsie Rolls, jujubes, chocolate cigarettes, and jelly beans of all colors, the red ones much in demand among those who dared to pretend to wear lipstick.

The day Auntie, going through my jumper before putting it into the laundry, came upon an unwrapped green leaf with a large bite out of it, my visits to the candy store came to an abrupt end. Not taken in by the lie I made up to explain where I'd got the candy, Auntie was convinced that I'd stolen money from a classmate. If I wouldn't tell her from whom, she'd take the matter to Miss Henderson, expose me to the whole class, to the principal if necessary. When I confessed about the milk money, I was not only lectured on the importance of milk and the danger of sweets to the growing body, with a vividly painted picture of what it would be like to be a toothless and brittle-boned adult, but was warned that if I didn't buy milk each day, the lunchroom teacher would call her at P.S. 10 and report it.

Until now it had never occurred to me to steal. The next time I was sent to the store to buy bread, my eyes lit on the open canister of chocolate-covered graham crackers that was on the counter. Summoning my courage, I asked what they cost. Two for a penny. I said I'd take two. On the way home I wolfed down the cookies. Putting the bread on the kitchen table and the change beside it, I went to my room to wait for trouble. None came that day, nor the next. When it did, and it didn't take long, the message that came through to me clearly was that for the dull-witted crime did not pay.

Had Auntie been less attentive, or I less timid, I might have gone on to more serious delinquency. But as a thief I showed little talent, and my lies, as Auntie derisively pointed out, were transparent and illuminated by guilty blushes. Thereafter I didn't go straight, but neither did I go on to bigger things. When a new teacher came to the lunchroom, I rationalized that instead of milk I could substitute a Milky Way. I ate the candy bar on the spot, so there would be no evidence such as there had been with the green leaf.

In the end a simple-minded form of protest turned out to be surprisingly effective. I stopped bathing. Stopped completely. When I should have been in the tub scrubbing myself, I sat on a bath stool in a fog of steam, wool-gathering. A fake splash or two, a resounding slosh, a dampened towel, and a crumpled bathmat were all that was needed to convince anyone, so I thought, that I had taken a bath. Had I been a boy no one would have been alarmed. Boys are allowed an unwashed period: Boys will be boys. But a dirty girl? Wasn't this a sign of *pathology?* wondered Auntie, who found me out before long.

I had begun the year as a nonreader who thought there was something wrong with her brain. The "something" felt, when I was calm enough to analyze it, like a mechanical failure: a switchboard with lines that had become scrambled. In moments of panic — during oral reading lessons — the mechanism broke down completely: Messages were neither sent nor delivered. By the end of the school year, the "something" had become so general that I was convinced I was defective both intellectually and morally. I was stupid. I was lazy. I was a liar. I was a petty thief. I was an awkward, accident-prone, slovenly, stooped, stuttering, dirty, crybaby.

Abruptly the evening lessons were canceled. The cause and nature of my backwardness were no longer discussed openly. (Indeed, it became an unmentionable.) At school the heat was off.

Was it, as I liked to think, if the word *think* can be used to describe a process so little conscious and articulated, that by not bathing I had shown Auntie and Miss Henderson that they had pushed me too far? Without comment, and for no reason that I could see other than that I was the tallest girl in the class, I was promoted — a "social" promotion it was called — to fifth grade.

From hell I was moving into a limbo of illiteracy.

Chapter III

When testing dyslexics as to their power of silent or oral reading, it is not infrequently found that the child performs no worse — sometimes even a little better — if the book is held upside down.

The Dyslexic Child, by Macdonald Critchley

Dyslexia (from the Greek, *dys*, faulty, + *lexis*, speech, cognate with the Latin *legere*, to read), developmental or specific dyslexia as it's technically called, the disorder I suffered from, is the inability of otherwise normal children to read. Children whose intelligence is below average, whose vision or hearing is defective, who have not had proper schooling, or who are too emotionally disturbed or brain-damaged to profit from it belong in other diagnostic categories. They, too, may be unable to learn to read, but they cannot properly be called dyslexics.

For more than seventy years the essential nature of the affliction has been hotly disputed by psychologists, neurologists, and educators. It is generally agreed, however, that it is the result of a neurophysiological flaw in the brain's ability to process language. It is probably inherited, although some experts are reluctant to say this because they fear people will equate "inherited" with "untreatable." Treatable it certainly is: not a disease to be cured, but a malfunction that requires retraining.

Reading is the most complex skill a child entering school is asked to develop. What makes it complex, in part, is that letters are less constant than objects. A car seen from a distance, close to, from above, or below, or in a mirror still looks like a car even though the optical image changes. The letters of the alphabet are more whimsical. Take the letter *b*. Turned upside down it becomes a *p*. Looked at in a mirror, it becomes a *d*. Capitalized, it becomes something quite different, a *B*. The *M* upside down is a *W*. The *E* flipped over becomes Ǝ. This reversed *E* is familiar to mothers of normal children who have just begun to go to school. The earliest examples of art work they bring home often have I LOVƎ YOU written on them.

Dyslexics differ from other children in that they read, spell, and write letters upside down and turned around far more frequently and for a much longer time. In what seems like a capricious manner, they also add letters, syllables, and words, or, just as capriciously, delete them. With palindromic words (was –saw, on –no), it is the order of the letters rather than the orientation they change. The new word makes sense, but not the sense intended. Then there are other words where the changed order — "sorty" for story — does not make sense at all.

The inability to recognize that g, *g*, and G are the same letter, the inability to maintain the orientation of the letters, to retain the order in which they appear, and to follow a line of text without jumping above or below it — all the results of the flaw — can make of an orderly page of words a dish of alphabet soup.

Also essential for reading is the ability to store words in memory and to retrieve them. This very particular kind of memory dyslexics lack. So, too, do they lack the ability to hear what the eye sees, and to see what they hear. If the eye sees "off," the ear must hear "off" and not "of," or "for." If the ear hears "saw," the eye must see that it looks like "saw" on the page and not "was." Lacking these skills, a sentence or paragraph becomes a coded message to which the dyslexic can't find the key.

It is only a slight exaggeration to say that those who learned to read without difficulty can best understand the labor reading is for a dyslexic by turning a page of text upside down and trying to decipher it.

While the literature is replete with illustrations of the way these children write and spell, there are surprisingly few examples of how they read. One, used for propaganda purposes to alert the public to the vulnerability of dyslexics in a literate society, is a sign warning that behind it are guard dogs trained to kill. The dyslexic reads:

Wurring
Guard God
Patoly

for

Warning
Guard Dog
Patrol

and, of course, remains ignorant of the danger.

Looking for a more commonplace example, and hoping to recapture the way I must have read in fourth grade, I recently observed dyslexic children at the Educational Therapy Clinic in Princeton, through the courtesy of Elizabeth Travers, the director. The first child I saw, eight-year-old Anna (whose red hair and brown eyes reminded me of myself at that age), had just come to the Clinic and was learning the alphabet. Given the story of "Little Red Riding Hood," which is at the second grade level, she began confidently enough, repeating the title from memory, then came to a dead stop. With much coaxing throughout, she read as follows:

> Grandma you a top. Grandma [looks over at picture of Red Riding Hood]. Red Riding Hood [long pause, presses index finger into the paper. Looks at me for help. I urge: Go ahead] the a [puts head close to the page, nose almost touching] on Grandma

for

> Once upon a time there was a little girl who had a red coat with a red hood. Etc.

"Grandma" was obviously a memory from having heard the story read aloud. Had I needed a reminder of how maddening my silences must have been to Miss Henderson, and how much patience is required to teach these children, Anna, who took almost ten minutes to read these few lines, furnished it. The main difference between Anna and me at that age is that Anna clearly felt no need to invent. She was perplexed, but not anxious, and seemed to have infinite tolerance for her long silences.

Toby, a nine-year-old boy with superior intelligence, had a year of tutoring behind him and could have managed "Little Red Riding Hood" with ease. His text was taken from the *Reader's Digest's Reading Skill Builder,* Grade IV. He read:

> A kangaroo likes as if he had but truck together warm. His saw neck and head do not . . . [Here Toby sighed with fatigue] seem to feel happy back. They and tried and so every a tiger likes Moses and shoots from lonesome day and shouts and long shore animals. And each farm play with five friends . . .

He broke off with the complaint, "This is too hard. Do I have to read any more?"

His text was:

> A kangaroo looks as if he had been put together wrong. His small neck and head do not seem to fit with his heavy back legs and thick tail. Soft eyes, a twinkly little nose and short front legs seem strange on such a large strong animal. And each front paw has five fingers, like a man's hand.

An English expert gives the following bizarre example of an adult dyslexic's performance:

> An the bee-what in the tel mother of the biothodoodoo to the majoram or that emidrate eni eni Krastrei, mestriet to Ketra lotombreidi to ra from treido as that.

His text, taken from a college catalogue the examiner happened to have close at hand, was:

> It shall be in the power of the college to examine or not every licentiate, previous to his admission to the fellowship, as they shall think fit.

That evening when I read aloud to Auntie for the first time, I probably began as Toby did, my memory of the classroom lesson keeping me close to the text. When memory ran out, and Auntie did not correct my errors, I began to invent. When she still didn't stop me, I may well have begun to improvise in the manner of this patient — anything to keep going and keep up the myth that I was reading — until Auntie brought the "gibberish" to a halt.

Until the end of the nineteenth century little attempt was made to separate the intelligent nonreader from mentally defective nonreaders. In a literate society, where intelligence and reading are closely associated in the minds of most people, it is not difficult to see why this should have been so. To complicate matters, nonreaders sooner or later begin to think of themselves as dull-witted. From there it is only a step to looking and acting dull-witted.

Nevertheless, perceptive teachers and parents must always have been baffled by children who, while clearly intelligent in other ways, could not be taught to read. If the student happened to be a royal prince who would one day be king, his tutor would have had to improvise methods of instructing him in history, geography, and whatever else he would have needed to know to perform his royal duties. It would be interesting to know how the tutors of Karl XI of Sweden (1655–1697), called "one of Sweden's wisest kings," managed, for we are told that Karl's progress in learning to read was extraordinarily slow. As an adult he remained so uncomfortable with the written word that he relied on oral reports. If handed a document, he pretended to read it, as often as not holding it upside down.

In a king such behavior is called eccentric. Other non-readers in literate families in Karl's day were probably called stupid and lazy. The best chance they had of being educated was to display a talent in a nonverbal area, like painting or architecture, in which case they might be given special training; or to have a teacher or parent who persisted in believing them to be educable despite evidence to the contrary.

It is not difficult to imagine the feelings of cultivated French bourgeois parents, such as Gustave Flaubert's, upon discovering they had a son who could not learn to read. Jean-Paul Sartre, in his three-volume study of Flaubert, *L'idiot de la famille*, says that when Gustave's mother, who had tried to teach him as she had taught her other children, failed, she turned the boy over to his father. A man of iron will, the father saw to it that by the time his son was ready to go off to school, at age nine, he was literate. Flaubert's early failure to understand that letters made syllables, and syllables words, which his sister, younger by three years, grasped without difficulty, and the humiliation he suffered during the lessons is, according to Sartre, the "deep wound, always hidden," that was too painful for Flaubert to talk about, or even write about openly.

This trauma, Sartre claims, gave Flaubert, who was as precocious a writer as he was retarded a reader, the subject for his early fiction. When he was fifteen, he wrote a novel, *Quidquid volueris*, in which a character named Djalioh, who is half-man, half-monkey, attracts the attention of scientists because he cannot learn to read. They try to teach him, in vain. Djalioh's brain — "narrow and compressed in front," which in the adolescent Flaubert's neuroanatomy was the seat of intelligence, "and at the back prodigiously developed," the seat of sensibility — cannot comprehend that the signs on the page stand for words. When examined by the scientists, Djalioh remains mute, not because he can't speak, but because he's afraid of making a mistake. Freak that he is, he nevertheless feels more than ordinary literate people do, but he is not examined on his sensibility and intuitiveness.

An even more touching story, if read in the light of Flaubert's early failure, is *Un parfum à sentir*. A father in a traveling circus tries to teach his sons how to walk a tightrope. When it's Ernesto's turn, he trembles with fear because he sees his father take up a whip. The father uses it to guide Ernesto, and to punish him if he makes a false step. By the time the boy has learned his lesson, there are traces of blood on the rope from the many whippings.

The genius of the man who would one day be hailed as one of the greatest poets of the twentieth century was also so little apparent when he was nine years old, and still couldn't read, that his family began to think of him as mentally defective:

> Several of my uncles and aunts had tried to teach me to read, and because they could not, and because I was much older than children who read easily, had come to think . . . that I had not all my faculties.

Thus in *Autobiographies* writes W. B. Yeats.

Had Yeats remained with his mother's family in the West of Ireland, he might have become merely a teller-of-tales in a country where the oral tradition is strong. His father, the painter John Butler Yeats, becoming concerned as time passed and the boy still didn't learn to read, decided to take him in hand. The poet, recalling this painful period in his life — in what is a unique account, remarkable for its candor — says his father was an impatient teacher who, in anger, threw the book at his head.

> The only lessons I had ever learned were those my father
> taught me, for he terrified me by descriptions of my moral
> degradation and he humiliated me by my likeness to dis-
> agreeable people.

As it turned out, it was not by being humiliated that Yeats
received the education necessary for a great poet, but by
another pedagogical technique his father eventually devised.

Twenty years later, in 1896, in the south of England, an
adolescent schoolboy named Percy, who was even more
backward in reading and spelling than Yeats, became the
subject of a ground-breaking article in the *British Medical
Journal*. Dr. Pringle Morgan examined Percy and found him
to be physically and mentally sound. Yet

> He did not read a single word correctly with the exception
> of 'and', 'the', 'of', 'that', etc. The other words seemed to
> be quite unknown to him and he could not even make an
> attempt to pronounce them.

When asked to write, Percy fared no better. His own name
he wrote as "Precy." Nonetheless, his schoolmaster reported
that had all the lessons been conducted orally Percy would
have been at the top of his class. Dr. Morgan, observing that
despite normal vision the boy seemed to have no power to
take in or store visual impressions of words, asked the question: "Could it be that there exists a condition which one
might call 'congenital word-blindness'?"

In subsequent years neurologists, reporting similar cases,
answered Morgan's question in the affirmative, but no full-
scale study of word-blind children and their educational
needs was made until the midtwenties when Samuel T.
Orton, an American neurologist and psychiatrist, appeared
on the scene. In the course of studying mental health problems in the state of Iowa, Orton discovered that among the
children reported by their teachers as dull and failing in

school, there was a fairly high proportion whose errors in reading and spelling were strikingly like those of the word-blind children reported on in British and American journals. In his first article, published in 1925, he used the word *strephosymbolia* — twisted symbols — to describe the phenomenon, preferring it to the term *word-blindness* because he observed that these children not only twisted letters and words they saw. They also twisted what they heard, what they wrote, and what they said. Orton recognized that dyslexia is not a single symptom; rather, it is a syndrome (a cluster of symptoms), which may include physical awkwardness, poor penmanship, hyperactivity, stuttering, directional disorientation, a weakness in visual memory, as well as the more familiar difficulties with spelling, writing, arithmetic, and, of course, reading.

Orton had published his paper by the time I was in 4A², and was developing his remedial techniques throughout the years of my schooling, but his work was known to only a small group of his students. Auntie, although very much interested in education, and particularly in how to educate me, had not heard of him. So she did what others before her who tried to teach dyslexics had done: Working in the dark, she tried first one technique and then another.

Although my backwardness was never again discussed openly, nor the oral reading lessons resumed after the year in Miss Henderson's class, only superficially had Auntie accepted defeat. In limbo, subtler and gentler pedagogical techniques were essayed. My resistance to books being what it was, Auntie turned elsewhere for teaching aids. Using printed words on billboards, signs in shop windows, and advertisements in subway cars, she tried to make a game, the "sign-game," of our reading them together.

"What's the man up there saying?" she'd ask, pointing to a billboard.

"Where?" I'd stall.

"He's saying: 'No more energy? Get a *lift* from a Camel.' Now, you say it."

Or, her eye catching the cardboard dummy of a fair-skinned beauty advertising Yardley's English Lavender in a drugstore window, she'd read out: "Complexion as Fair as an English June."

Or, in the subway, above the straps, the Wrigley's chewing gum ad: "Yoo Hoo! Don't forget the Double Mint!"

"Yoo Hoo," I'd repeat, playing the game dispiritedly. Cod liver oil was cod liver oil; no amount of orange juice could disguise it or make it more palatable. Nevertheless, every once in a while the spelling of a word would strike me. "So *that's* how 'yoo hoo' looks," I'd say to myself in wonder.

There was one sign I passed almost every day that intrigued me. It was the movie marquee outside Loew's Inwood on Dyckman Street. On winter afternoons I loved the way the lights twinkled in the growing dark. One day I saw the man from the ticket window come out with a ladder and a box full of letters made of metal. With a single letter in his hand at a time, he climbed the ladder and built a word, then another, until he had a title. Thinking, confusedly, that the titles were his invention, I wondered if he thought them up ahead of time or made them up as he went along.

Since Marie and I were not allowed to go to the Saturday matinee with the other children in the neighborhood, movies had the allure of the forbidden. The Inwood movies must be very different from the slapstick comedies and Tom Mix Westerns — pies, pratfalls, thundering horses, smoking guns — we had been shown once a week at Farmingdale. If they were not wicked, why this prohibition against them? One day I came home and volunteered the information that "Gemperblond" was playing. Only the initiated would have been able to decode that what I meant was *Gentlemen Prefer Blondes*. Auntie and Aunt Lucy laughed as they unscrambled the title — but wait, Auntie said, suddenly serious, wasn't this the first time I'd attempted to read a sign on my own? It gave her an idea for another pedagogical device.

Every evening from then on, I was given a list of the items needed for the evening meal, the shopping Auntie ordinarily did on her way home from Harlem, and was sent to Dyckman Street. This would force me to learn the words on the list and stimulate me to read signs along the way. At first, seeing this new chore as a disguised punishment, I dragged my feet, dawdled en route. Once, failing to look both ways as I'd been taught, I ran into the street and was hit by a car. I was picked up by the bumper and tossed to the other side of the street, where I landed, in a state of shock but in one piece. Knowing that I was in the wrong, I scrambled up and hurried about my errands, intending not to mention the accident at home. When I returned I found the driver (who had questioned the neighbors about where I lived) waiting for me with Auntie. She was both apprehensive and angry.

"Are you trying to get yourself *killed?*" she demanded. "Why didn't you look where you were going?"

I didn't know why. My carelessness had alarmed me at least as much as it alarmed her. How could I have walked right in front of an oncoming car?

The driver and Auntie hustled me off to a nearby hospital, where I was x-rayed, my bruises cleaned and dressed. Once home, I was told how lucky I was to have escaped without a fracture, or worse, and was punished for my heedlessness. For some time thereafter I crossed streets with great care, not because of the punishment but because I didn't trust myself.

To my surprise, before long I began to look forward to these solitary outings. In the early evening light, Dyckman Street, the main street of Inwood, took on the glamor of a bazaar. I liked to lose myself among the throngs of office workers who poured out of the subway and hurried through their errands, eager to get home at the end of the day. I pretended that I, too, was grown up, independent — what a thrill the word gave me! — that I was buying not what was on my list but whatever I chose to make up an unbalanced and mouth-watering meal. Each shop I went into had its own aroma, its own decor. The stationery and newspaper store, a dim, crowded place with a backroom that was filled with toys for sale at Christmas time, smelled of Cuban cigars and Turkish tobacco, cozy, masculine odors missing from our feminine household. When I grew up I would smoke Murads that came in a flat tin box, as my father had done.

The shiny, tiled bakery next door was fragrant with bread, buns, and cakes which were, as I knew from having repeated it after Auntie, "baked on the premises." The Jewish dairy was my favorite store and the one I had most occasion to visit during this period. Brilliant overhead lights shone down on tubs of sweet and salt butter, plump curds of pot cheese, barrels of dill pickles, crates of brown and white eggs, baskets of kosher soap stamped with Hebrew letters in gaudy runny colors. Their exotic appearance, which helped me to distinguish them from English letters, aroused my curiosity. What did they say? On the white marble counter were great rounds of brown bread sold by the pound, paper bags of onion rolls and bagels. On a cutting board were bars of marbled and pistachio-studded halvah. Behind the counter were men, dressed alike in white aprons, their shirt sleeves rolled up, exposing chapped red hands and muscular forearms. They were constantly in motion, weighing, cutting, wrapping, shouting, clowning, teasing, flirting with the customers. "What's yours, young lady?" they'd ask me, playing into my fantasy of being grown up. As they got to know me better, they called me "Sweetheart," "Doll," "Honey," "Redhead," "Little Darling," appellations that fell sweetly on my ear. They petted me, praised me, fed me tidbits, asked me if I would like to go home with them, be their little girl. If, during vacations, it was Uncle Charlie's admiration and approval that gave a much needed lift to my low view of myself, day-to-day it was the dairy men who performed the same service. Their flattery, which they dealt out as generously as they dealt out the pot cheese, was as nourishing to the psyche as their dairy products were to the body.

Laden down with sweet butter, eggs, and cream, I continued on my errands. The lights of the marquee at Loew's Inwood beckoned me to the theater. The stills of the Saturday cliffhanger showed a train bearing down with murderous velocity on a disheveled woman whose eyes bulged with fright. What happened to her? Did she get away in time?

The seductions of Loew's Inwood proved irresistible. My sister, my daring sister, who had been fighting the restriction against movies, had been urging me to go with her "on the sneak." All our friends went every Saturday afternoon; why couldn't we? The Saturday *Wild Orchids* was playing we joined the queue with our friends, walked through the lobby, carpeted richly in ruby red, and took our seats under the star-studded midnight-blue sky. On the silver screen a half-dressed and languid lady appeared. She slunk around a Javanese prince who wore only pajamas. *Silk* pajamas. Was the lady good or bad? Marie, who was spellbound, whispered that she'd explain it to me later. When the Prince de Gace (for that was his name) tossed the siren onto a couch strewn with satin pillows and covered her with kisses, I grasped the meaning of a word I'd been curious about since the days of my catechism lessons at Dobbs Ferry. It was one of the results of original sin. Since the nun who prepared me for my confirmation gave it a sibilant, sultry sound when she pronounced it, and was evasive when I asked its meaning, the unanswered question had remained in my mind. The sneak visit to the movies, while Auntie would not have approved of it, turned out to be one of the most successful lessons. Greta Garbo and Nils Asther taught me, as no dictionary could have done, the meaning of a word well above my grade level: "concupiscence."

Chapter IV

I missed [my nurse] terribly. Every day I wrote her — a short, badly written ill-spelled note: writing and spelling were always terribly difficult for me. My letters were without originality.

Every day I had to learn how to spell pages of words. I suppose this exercise did me some good, but I was still an extraordinarily bad speller, and have remained so until the present day.

I myself was always recognized, though quite kindly, as "the slow one" of the family . . . It was quite true, and I knew it and accepted it.

An Autobiography, by Agatha Christie (author of 68 novels, 100 short stories, and 17 plays)

It would be a mistake to think, as I did at the time, that I had learned nothing in 4A^2 or from the evening lessons. Painful as they were, they were also instructive. Both my teachers underestimated my progress, and led me to do so, because the only way they thought to test me was by having me read aloud. Silent reading, a less demanding skill, was considerably easier for me. It permitted me time to trace the outline of a letter with my reading finger. Miss Henderson's repeated corrections:

It's *d* not *p*. Say it: *d d d*
d d d I'd say

may finally have sunk in, but my way, which I hit on by accident, was even more useful. I had learned that *d* felt one way, *p* another, from tracing them. Kinesthesia, the feel of my muscles as my arm moved up or down, was what I relied on, not visual memory or learning by rote.

Silent reading also allowed me to move back and forth along a line of print at my own pace, and in my own way, instead of in the smooth and more rapid manner my auditors demanded. Best of all, I did not have to concern myself with an audience, which meant that energy liberated when there was no need to brace myself for ridicule could be used to decode the symbols. Decoding symbols — seeing "apple" and understanding that a–p–p–l–e was the word I knew for a round, red fruit I was extremely familiar with — remained the great stumbling block to reading.

While oral reading holds its terrors for me to this day, by the end of fourth grade I was reading silently well enough to decode some words and string them into sentences. Given the nursery rhyme "Jack and Jill," for example, I would have made something like this out of it:

> Jack and Jill
> Went up the hill
> To ? a ? of water
> Jack fell down
> And broke his ?
> And Jill came ? after.

A combination of lack of self-confidence and a powerful resistance to written words would have kept me from attempting to fill in the question marks. And I would have been so busy working on the passage, and so fatigued from the effort, that I would not have paid attention to what the nursery rhyme was about.

In fifth grade, the benign period of the "sign-game," I began to fill in the blanks — sometimes with the word-attack method Miss Henderson had favored, in which one did not attempt the whole word but separated it into parts and attacked each of them:

> To fe   etch a

Or, if that didn't tell me anything, and it often didn't, I would have fallen back on guesswork, but a more reasoned guesswork than formerly:

> *To fe   etch* . . . what kind of a word is that? It must be to "get." *To get a pal of water.* What's a pal? A bucket of water.

Ignoring the rhyme, and the help it could have given me, I would have had Jack break his *neck.* Jill would have come *running* after.

Not a precise reading certainly; rather, a free translation.

Those who learned to read English without difficulty can best imagine the process by recalling the way they worked out a translation when they began a second language.

To my great relief, to my great joy, oral reading disappeared from the syllabus in fifth grade. And with its disappearance my reading grade rose from a failure to a 65: passing, but only just. My new teacher seemed to be much more interested in her students' conduct than in their intellectual performance. She valued highly my ability to sit still, to control the temptation to whisper to my neighbor, and to keep my eyes resolutely on her in the front of the room when a visitor entered the classroom by the rear door — disciplines I'd learned from the nuns at Dobbs Ferry. Once again I found myself in the familiar and comfortable role of "good girl."

At home there was a gradual shift in attitude toward my affliction, as the laughter over "Gemperblond" showed. What had been a cause for great anxiety, when threatening letters accompanied report cards, now became (at least on the surface) a family joke. Minor symptoms, which had their "comical" side — an inability to control what I wanted to say, confusion over handedness, awkwardness — attracted more attention. The pain didn't go away with this shift. It merely moved to another zone where it throbbed and burned, until quite by chance I made an invaluable discovery.

If, when I made a slip of the tongue, I put on a droll expression, or if, when I made an awkward gesture, I gave it a Chaplinesque flourish, my audience ceased mocking and began applauding. This act was not easy to bring off. It required alertness (for which I was not famous), as well as timing and practice. Above all, it was essential to suppress the sense of shock I felt at each fresh bit of evidence that my skull housed an unruly brain. Instead of being astonished to have said, "The birds are losing their leaves" (when what I meant, of course, was that they were losing their feathers), I had to catch the cue from my interlocutors' expression that what I had said was ludicrous and pretend to have said it on purpose. Instead of blushing with confusion to have extended my left instead of my right to shake hands, I had to make my left hand describe an amusing arabesque in the air as if it had been a mere preparation for presenting the right. The first time I brought it off Aunt Lucy said, "You are a sketch!"

To be a sketch was greatly preferable to being the family idiot. Encouraged, I tried out my act in school. What had made Aunt Lucy smile ruefully made my classmates, always greedy for a diversion, explode with laughter. The same boys and girls who the previous year had laughed at the freak were now laughing with the jester. The teacher clapped her hands and said, "Class! Class!" calling it to order, but she was laughing too. It wasn't long before I was acknowledged to be the class clown.

A side effect of my clowning, as agreeable as it was unpredictable, was that I became popular. Until Miss Henderson's class I had always got on well with other children, but I had not thought of myself as popular. (If the concept existed at Dobbs Ferry or Farmingdale I had been unaware of it.) At P.S. 52, to be popular was very, very important. It gave one more status than having a good character, being pretty, rich, athletic, or even intelligent. I began to be sought after in the lunchroom. I never lacked for companions on the walk home from school. Girls asked to be my "best friend," and boys began to treat me like a pal and invited me to play games with them in the school yard. I became something of a tomboy. Nothing gave me greater pleasure, apart from dancing (for which at that age my only partner was my sister), than running, jumping, throwing a ball. Even here there were problems. Did I throw with the right or left? (Over with the left, under with the right.) On which side did I hold the bat? These uncertainties made it unlikely that I would ever be a good athlete, but at the fifth grade level, where there were only informal teams, my enthusiasm more than made up for a lack of skill.

My sister, whose opinion mattered greatly to me, disapproved of these sweaty games and the way I "wasted" my free time. Although each of us was still the other's best friend, a powerful wedge had been driven between us since we'd entered public school. As we were discovering, the literate and illiterate inhabit different worlds. In Marie's world, learning and order were sought after; in mine, action and anarchy. It showed up in little things. The clothes closet we shared became a bone of contention between us. On the floor on my sister's side, highly polished shoes, boots, rubbers were paired off like soldiers ready for inspection. On my side they were covered with dust or mud, depending on the season, and lay scattered and buried under a welter of athletic equipment. While I was running around the school yard getting overheated, ripping and dirtying my dresses, Marie was sitting in the local branch of the public library, cool and kempt, reading. Instead of playing in the school yard, why didn't I come to the library with her? Only on Saturdays when the weather made outdoor play impossible could she drag me with her.

As I crossed the threshold of the Inwood Public Library and saw the children frozen in rigid postures, eyes glued to the page, or with self-important airs looking up words in a giant dictionary, or whispering conspiratorially with the librarian, I became as guarded and suspicious as a savage approaching alien territory. The very odor of the place, compounded of mildew, library paste, and feet in overshoes, made my stomach turn over. The thought that for hours, until Marie was ready to leave, I would be trapped in this dreary environment surrounded by books, loathsome books, made my spirits sag, my shoulders slump, my eyes go vacant.

In an effort to rouse me out of my stupor and interest me in her favorite pastime, Marie would select "something easy" for me to read from *The Rose Fairy Book* or one of the others in Andrew Lang's series to which other ten-year-olds were addicted. Turning to a story she remembered with excitement, she'd say, "Here!" as if I could not fail to be carried away and, opening her own book, re-enter a trancelike state.

Outside (outside being whatever was not home, school, or the library), where I limited myself to the kind of printed matter my school-yard pals and I favored, I read well enough to satisfy my modest needs: to follow the comic strip, "Mandrake the Magician"; to understand the jokes accompanying cartoons I saw in battered magazines in the dentist's office, and, from the same provenance, advertisements for Djer Kiss face powder and other (forbidden) cosmetics, samples of which one could write away for; to learn the words of popular songs from tabloid-sized songsheets printed on luridly colored paper.

While I had only a limited interest in knowing what part of the body Jack broke, I had to have the lyrics of popular songs *just* right. If I slipped up on the words of that tongue-twister

> I miss
> My Swiss
> My Swiss miss
> misses me

my playmates, who were in this regard semantic pedants, would have been disdainful.

If I limited myself to "junk" literature, and only that part of it, like "Mandrake," that was in vogue with my friends, I was able to convince myself that I read as well as any other ten-year-old. Books, especially library books, forced me to face the truth. I responded to the Inwood Public Library as to an allergen. My body acted up in the strangest ways. It needed water to slake an imperious thirst. I went to the drinking fountain in the hall. Drank copiously. Played with the start-and-stop button. Chatted with another escapee. Dawdled on the way back to my seat. Having taken in the water, my system became impatient to eliminate it. I climbed the stairs to the second floor. Emptied my bladder. Washed my hands as carefully as a surgeon. Played with the soap dispenser. Catching my image in the mirror, I practiced making faces for my clown act. I wiggled my ears, tried to make one eyebrow go up, the other down, let my jaw go slack for my stupid look. I gazed out of the window, wondered what my school-yard friends were up to. Back in the reading room my stomach announced that it was empty. Shouldn't we go? I whispered to my sister. She shook her head disapprovingly: We had just arrived. I was hungry. My stomach was growling. It kept me from concentrating. Marie was showing signs of vexation. She cared more about her dumb old books than about her only sister.

Pretending I had come across a word I needed to look up, I slipped out of my chair and went to the dictionary. There was a secret list of words (of which "concupiscence" had been one) I carried around in my head that I was genuinely curious about. "Breasts," for example. It was not easy to find. As few adults seemed to realize, to be able to look up a word, one had to know how to spell it: brsts? braest? Was it one of those *really* tricky words which begin with an unpronounced letter? No, here it was: "breasts: milk-secreting organs in woman." Dictionaries were always disappointing. I didn't want to know what breasts did. My question was, when would I have them?

"Womb: organ in woman in which child or young is conceived." What did *that* mean? The Virgin "conceived" but that was a miracle.

"Conceive: to become pre . . ." The snoopy librarian came up behind me, pretending she wanted to look up a word when what she was really doing was checking up on me. I blushed, slammed the dictionary closed, and returned to my seat.

Why had Marie pretended that this story was an easy one? It was called, "What the Rose Said to the ___?___." Leaning over to her, my finger on the word I didn't recognize, I asked, "To the what?"

" 'The Cypress.' You mean to say you haven't read any farther than *that?*"

If Marie was going to be critical, I wouldn't ask her for help anymore.

> Once upon a time a great king of the East named ___?___
> had three brave and clever sons ___?___, ___?___, and ___?___.

After a page or two of skipping unpronounceable names and hard words, I couldn't remember the familial relationships between Sama-tal-posh, Tehmasp, Qamas, and Almas-ruh-bakhsh, and didn't care how brave and clever they were or what happened to them. Had someone read fairy tales to me I would undoubtedly have enjoyed them. To have been motivated to read one on my own, I would have required a tale that came closer to home. One about a simpleton who couldn't learn to read until a clever medicine man came to the kingdom and, touching her on the head with his magic wand, cured her, would have done nicely.

Why did they call this series the "rose," the "green," "blue," "crimson," "yellow," or "violet" book when they all wore the same dull library binding? They had few color illustrations, and the black-and-white line drawings were more black than white, reminding me of the Whirligig reader and the sore-to-the-touch recent past. After a while the excessive heat in the reading room, the stale air, the dancing lines of print, and my mounting frustration acted as a soporific. I fell into an uneasy, escapist sleep.

At closing time, my sister would gather up an armful of books, enough to last her until the following Saturday, and take them to the check-out desk. Empty handed, I sidled out behind her, my library card *virgo intacto.* I didn't always get past the beady-eyed librarian with the dyed black hair. If she caught me, she would put her face so close to mine I could smell the breath I thought probably came from spending so many hours in a library, and insist that there must be at least one book I would like to take home. I had forgotten my library card, I would say, backing away. Or, I had a book at home. Or, letting my jaw go slack, I'd pretend I hadn't understood. In the end, succumbing to her bullying, for she kept after me relentlessly, I charged out, one at a time, *Heidi, The Secret Garden, Pinocchio, Lad, Anne of Green Gables, Rebecca of Sunnybrook Farm, Treasure Island, Black Beauty, The Adventures of Tom Sawyer, A Tale of Two Cities, Three Musketeers, Kim, The Swiss Family Robinson, The Jungle Book,* and *Gulliver's Travels* and returned them the next rainy Saturday, unread.

Miss Shapiro, my sixth grade teacher, I often suspected had spies in the library, for she blamed my poor spelling on my lack of "outside reading." It was a mystery to her how I'd reached her grade, spelling as I did. The mystery to me was how others knew what order to put the letters in. Had all spelling been taught by rules, in jingles one could learn by rote, such as

> Write *i* before *e*
> Except after *c*
> Or when sounded as *a*
> As in *neighbor* and *weigh*

I would have been able to manage far better than I did. Better, but still not well. The jingle helped me to spell "niece" (an important word for me — I was a niece many times over and had to sign myself "Your loving niece" in thank-you letters for birthday and Christmas gifts), but it didn't keep me from transposing letters ("nad" for "and"), adding and subtracting others ("bfore" for "before"), or adding and subtracting syllables ("examimine" for "examine"). My memory, which served me well in some ways, was no help in spelling. I seemed not to be able to recall the way a word looked. Even when I happened to spell a word correctly, it often looked wrong, so I doctored it to make it look right. "Dear" looked incomplete to me, so I added a final "e."

If Miss Shapiro appreciated my good behavior and was amused by my clowning, she was blinded by neither. Where I had been able to fool my fifth grade teacher by writing a letter which could stand for "a," "i," or "e" when I was in doubt about what the vowel should be, Miss Shapiro would encircle the equivocal penmanship and put an X next to the word. As she often said, one had to get up early in the morning to fool her.

The long list of failed words from spelling tests I took home at the beginning of Christmas vacation, each to be rewritten fifty times, I had made little progress on before I came down with the flu. When I returned to school six weeks later, the list in hand, Miss Shapiro said,

"So you're back at last. Convalescence is an ideal time for reading. Come tell the class what books you've read."

Convalescence had been a very trying time for me. After the first two weeks I had been sure I was well enough to go out to play, but my fever chart had said I wasn't. Marie, who also had the flu, had been quite content to read, and had prodded me to follow her example. Some of the books I'd charged out of the Inwood Library, and had returned unread, mysteriously reappeared on the table with the vase of sweet peas and the glass that held the thermometer. It was either the spelling words to write,

examine
examine
examine
examine

until inattentiveness made it again

examimine

which I copied over and over, reinforcing my error. Or books. In desperation I turned to them. The one with the fewest pages and the most pictures was the one I settled on.

"Uh . . . It was a red book . . ." I said, answering Miss Shapiro's question.

"Go on."

"It was about a girl who lived in Switzerland . . ."

" 'A red book. A girl who lived in Switzerland.' What kind of a way is that to answer? What's the title of the book? Who is the author?"

Teachers were never satisfied. Why wouldn't Miss Shapiro just let me tell the story?

"It's *Heidi*," called out a prompter.

Yes, that was it, *Heidi*.

Dorothy, a show-offy bright girl, pointed out contemptuously that *Heidi* was a third grade book.

"And what else did you read?" Miss Shapiro coaxed, silencing the show-off.

There was another possibility I could mention. Marie had pressed it on me. Attracted by the title, *The Secret Garden*, I had drifted in and out of its pages, looking for the secret in a vague, feverish way, interested, yet not able to get a grip on the story. If I said I'd read it, Miss Shapiro would be pleased that I had noted the title, if not the author's name. However, she was sure to ask me that disconcerting question: What was it about? I could no more have said what it was about than I could have said what a cloud was about — which didn't keep me from looking at clouds, but how to put that across to Miss Shapiro? Better not mention it.

"Six weeks at home and that's *all* you've read! Don't you realize how important reading is for improving your spelling? You can't go to seventh grade spelling like a third grader. You don't want to be left back, do you?"

If there was anything that could have made me nostalgic for the days of confinement when, with feverish brow pressed against the icy windowpane, I had watched my friends down on the street throw snowballs or, with sleds under their arms, head toward Fort George for an afternoon of tobogganing, it was this threat of being left back. How could I, who at the best of times limped along behind the class like a lame dog behind a wagon, possibly catch up now?

I tried. Even more, I worried. If, by staying after school two afternoons a week, I could make up enough arithmetic to pass, I knew there was no possible way I could catch up in spelling, and Miss Shapiro's pep talks about "trying hard" only discouraged me further. The enormous and enervating effort I had made after the threat of being left back made my head feel as it had when I was coming down with the flu. What was the use? I'd ask myself when another Friday exam paper was returned with eight words wrong out of ten. After a while I gave up worrying about how far ahead the class was and concentrated instead on my relative position vis-à-vis Brontislava, the newly arrived Latvian girl. If I tried extra, extra hard to memorize words for the Friday tests, it was because the previous week Brontislava had made fewer mistakes than I, and I was afraid she and I would change positions, and I would again be at the bottom of the class.

At a moment when there was little reason to feel encouraged, I had an experience so startling, so inexplicable, that I kept it a secret, even from Marie. During an oral arithmetic test, as Miss Shapiro called out digits to be added, subtracted, multiplied, and divided, I became aware of a certain ease in making the calculations. My brain was working. I could *feel* it. My pleasure in doing the computations was as satisfying as sinking a basketball into the basket, as exhilarating — and as frightening — as flying down Fort George hill on a sled. Once, twice, three times, I steered my way over the treacherous surface, around the dangerous hazards (Miss Shapiro's combinations were famous for their sneaky traps), and landed safely. It took considerable restraint to control my euphoria, to keep from crying out, "Wheeeeeeee!"

What did it mean? I wondered. A fear that it would never happen again, and that if I reported it more would be expected of me — "You see? You can do it if you *really* try" — made me keep my tiny triumph to myself. It was good that I had, for it did not portend a growing facility with school work. Spelling remained as perplexing as ever. Arithmetic problems that had to be read were no easier to solve. My reading comprehension was no better than it had been.

Whether Miss Shapiro noticed my small breakthrough I don't know. At the time I thought she must have: Why else would she have promoted me? In the report she wrote for the school to which Marie and I were going to be transferred in the fall, she praised my good conduct and played down my borderline grades in reading and spelling, the result, she said charitably, of my long illness and absence from class.

The last day of school, as I said good-bye, jubilant not to have been left back, she asked to speak to me a moment after the other children had left. I knew I had just squeaked by, didn't I?

I nodded.

The new school I was going to had very high standards. It would not be easy for me there. The best way to prepare myself for the coming year was to read as much as I could during vacation. Would I promise her I would do that?

Again I nodded. But the moment I was out on the street, I uncrossed my fingers. How could she ask me to make such a promise? Read *on vacation?*

Chapter V

My mother offered me ten shillings if I would read a book. I tried to get through *Black Beauty* . . . I worked away at it alone and with the governess month after month. I made a little 'V' on the page to show how far I had got. I never finished the book, or, of course, received the ten shillings and *Black Beauty* is a nightmare to me.

From an anonymous account by a dyslexic Englishwoman who signed herself "X," in *The Dyslexic Child*, by Macdonald Critchley

Summer, my favorite season, meant freedom from my chronic anxiety about school. The fall would bring with it the usual apprehensiveness — What would my teacher's attitude toward the problem be? What kind of report cards would I take home? Would I be promoted, or instead of the usual and incomprehensible cliffhanger rescue, would I be left back? — but for two months at the beach I swam and played like other children, with hardly a reminder that there was anything wrong with me.

The summer I turned twelve, instead of going to Long Island with Auntie and our cousins as we usually did, Marie and I went to New Hampshire to visit distant relatives. Aunt Helen met us at White River Junction and drove us to Hanover. On a tree-lined street, she drew up before a white clapboard house where, in term time, students boarded. With "the boys," as they were called, away until September the comfortable old house, which had rooms of all sizes and shapes, as well as countless landings, doors, halls, stairs, cubbyholes, clothes presses, and closets, had more than enough space for two summer visitors. The large room in the front of the house, where Marie and I were installed, was furnished with a high four-poster bed, a Morris chair, and bookcases crammed with dog-eared textbooks. Above the bookcase hung a pair of snowshoes. In the corner there was a roll-top desk, said to contain a secret compartment, on which stood an iron inkwell and a wooden pipe stand. An odor of tobacco clung to the room, giving off an elusive aura of masculinity.

A masculine aura hung over the whole town, a town whose center of activity was the men who attended Dartmouth.

With the college closed for the summer, Hanover's sleepy beauty, its giant elms, its Green crisscrossed with paths, its velvety lawns, its Colonial houses with window shades precisely drawn, its bell tower chimes which periodically broke the silence, all seemed to be waiting for the princes to return, to stir it to life again. Greek letters over the doors of the fraternity houses, which even Aunt Helen didn't know the meaning of, stories of initiations and secret passwords, of proms and carnivals, added to the mystery and romance.

In Baker Library, which we visited on our tour that first day, there was a portrait of Eleazer Wheelock, founder of the college, who, according to the words of the song, "went into the wilderness to teach the Indian." The reading room was strikingly different from the one in our proletarian public library. Volumes bound in plum and chocolate and wintergreen leather lined the walls. One didn't have to be interested in reading to respond to their mouth-watering colors. Oriental carpets covered the floors. In the browsing room there was a giant fireplace and alcoves with wingback chairs. How cozy it would be to curl up in one of these chairs before a roaring fire, to doze or daydream on a snowy winter day!

What must the town be like in winter? The boys would be everywhere, loitering on the Green, hurrying to class, studying in the library, drinking and dancing at the fraternity house. Wisdom. Mystery. Romance. Like a girl in love for the first time, I felt stirrings I didn't understand. I, who hated books and was impatient for school to be let out, had fallen in love — head over heels in love with academia.

As we were getting ready for bed that night, a time when we often exchanged confidences, I told Marie two momentous decisions I'd made during the day: When I grew up I would go to college. Yes, and afterward I would marry a professor and live in a town like Hanover.

Marie had been waiting for just such an opening. Earlier, when we'd been unpacking, she'd handed me the book she'd read on the train and said I must read it. I really would love it.

"Read *on vacation?*" Sometimes, as I told Marie, she sounded like Miss Shapiro. Didn't Marie realize how I was looking forward to getting away from everything connected with school? When we returned to the city . . . maybe . . . I half promised.

"No, you must read it now. How do you think you'll get into college if you can't read?" Marie asked after my astonishing announcement about my plans for the future.

Wounded, I said that I could so read.

"Sure. The funny papers."

A quarrel was brewing. Marie's patience had come to an end. Those Saturdays at the Inwood Library I'd made a terrible nuisance of myself. I preferred to play dopey games with boys rather than read companionably with her. During our convalescence I'd read only one book, one *baby* book. Who wanted to discuss *Heidi?* What good was it to have a sister if you couldn't discuss books with her?

Marie's reproaches stung me. Although I was even-tempered and said to have a "sunny disposition," unquestionably I was an imperfect companion. My side of the closet was always messy. At home when my feelings were hurt by ridicule, I cried, instead of presenting a stoical and dignified façade as Marie did when she was punished. I was too timid to keep up with her adventurousness. Until now I hadn't realized that one of the pleasures of reading was to "discuss" what you'd read with another.

"If you don't read this book, I won't speak to you all summer," she threatened.

"At all?"

"Not a single solitary word."

Marie had a terrible way of meaning what she said. Once or twice before when we'd had a disagreement she hadn't spoken to me. At such times, dreadful times, her silence had lasted at most an hour. A summer of silence I didn't like to imagine. Had she threatened me in the city I would have tried to bluff her out with a see-if-I-care-I'll-play-with-so-and-so attitude, for on Academy Street I never lacked companions. In Hanover, as she well knew, I was friendless.

"Besides," Marie said, "you really *will* love it." Her eyes misted over the way they did when she talked about books. "It's a wonderful story. You might at least take a look at it."

I extended my hand reluctantly to take the book from her. It was heavy. Worse, it was fat. The binding was a drab green. The title was written in gold lettering so florid the words were lost in a thicket of curlicues. A frontispiece showed four girls in old-fashioned dresses with leg-of-mutton sleeves, standing around a piano singing.

"What's it about?" I asked suspiciously.

"Sisters," my sister said, baiting the hook.

A promising subject, I had to admit. I turned to the first page. The title of the chapter, also written in fancy letters, was as incomprehensible to me as if it were in German script. The myth that I could read exploded in my face again. I spluttered, "I can't, I can't . . ." Marie was right: How had I dared dream of going to college? I probably wouldn't get into high school, or if I did, I'd be shunted into the commercial course. Nobody who took the commercial course ever married a professor, I felt sure. Sitting on the bed, my back to Marie, I covered my face with my hands.

"I'll begin it for you," Marie said, determined not to be moved by my tears. "You'll see, you won't be able to put it down."

Chapter One: Playing Pilgrims

"Christmas won't be Christmas without any presents," grumbled Jo, lying on the rug.

"It's so dreadful to be poor!" sighed Meg, looking down at her old dress.

"I don't think it's fair for some girls to have plenty of
pretty things, and other girls nothing at all," added little
Amy, with an injured sniff.
"We've got father and mother and each other," said Beth
contentedly from her corner.

I had stopped crying and was listening, spellbound less by
what Marie was reading than by her ease in making the dead
words come alive. In her voice Jo, Meg, Amy, and Beth became real people.

The four young faces on which the firelight shone bright-
ened at the cheerful words, but darkened again as Jo said
sadly:
"We haven't got father, and shall not have him for a long
time." She didn't say "perhaps never," but each silently
added it, thinking of father far away, where the fighting
was.

To be read to was a rare treat. In our family the practice of
reading aloud had died out with the death of my grandfather. Auntie had never read to us, probably because she considered us too old for it by the time we went to live with her.
At Farmingdale Miss Barnes had read to the class from time
to time — stories like *Hans Brinker* — not nearly as often as I
would have liked. And at Dobbs Ferry the only time I had
been read to was when I was in the infirmary. In the late afternoon when the nun who was my nurse had finished her
chores, she would sometimes read to me from what she
called "The Book." It contained not fairy tales about prin-
cesses and witches, but the real and sometimes blood-
curdling lives of the saints. She had her favorites. I had mine.
I begged to hear about Saint Patrick, who had left the civi-
lized world to trod the misty moonscape of a viper-ridden
island (where, improbable as it seemed, the nun told me my
ancestors had lived). My temperature rose and my toes

curled under the blanket as she described, improvising on the text, how Saint Patrick's naked feet narrowly escaped poisonous snake bite after bite.

Neither Miss Barnes nor my nurse read as well as Marie. I lay on the bed, my arms folded under my head, and drank it in. I was sorry when Aunt Helen, checking to see if we were in bed, told Marie to close the book and put out the light. We must go straight to sleep, she said. It had been a big day.

It had indeed. I had taken two giant steps toward a cure. I had decided, for spurious reasons to be sure, that I wanted to go to college. And to please my sister, I had agreed to read *Little Women*.

Rainy days in Hanover were reading days. If the sun was out, Marie was as happy as I was to go off with our new friends, bicycling, picnicking, swimming, or climbing in the foothills of the White Mountains. But when it rained, she held me to my promise. Dawdle as I might over breakfast, I could not put off indefinitely the moment when I would have to find the green book and accompany her to Baker Library. Under the indulgent eye of the librarian, an old school chum of Aunt Helen's, we tiptoed past the card catalogue and into the empty browsing room. Seated in a wingback chair, I took up the battle.

The characters that had been so clearly delineated in Marie's voice grew fuzzy as soon as I was on my own. Who was talking now? Was it Meg or Jo? The sisters, introduced one after the other, prattled on for pages before the author told me what they looked like. When she did, it was with this jolting intrusion:

> As young readers like to know "how people look," we will take this moment to give them a little sketch of the four sisters . . .

It required a push to fight past the patronizing sound of that grown-up voice to find out what they looked like. Meg, it seemed, was pretty, plump, and fair. Jo was tall, thin, and brown. Beth, rosy, smooth-haired, and not so bright.

Was it the thin, brown one speaking now? I wondered as the sisters started talking again. Or was it the rosy, smooth-haired one? The author didn't tell me. And was it worth the effort to find out when the story was so *dreary?*

Marie turned a deaf ear to my complaints. I was just making excuses. I had promised, remember? If the threat that she wouldn't speak to me was the stick, the carrot she held in front of me was that in a few pages a male figure would be introduced into this entirely female household. And Meg and Jo would go to a dance. So prodded, teased, encouraged, threatened, I slogged my way from chapter to chapter.

There was a revenge I could take, I discovered, against the author, the enemy who had strung together so many thousands of sentences: I could skip. I skipped and I skipped. Descriptions, especially of nature. Poetry, of which Louisa May was inordinately fond,

> Hither, hither, from thy home,
> Airy sprite, I bid thee come!
> Born of roses, fed on dew,
> Charms and potions canst thou brew?

etc., out! Playlettes. Dreams. Letters. Diary notes. Anything that could be classified as unnecessary filler, slowing down the pace which I would have moved at breakneck speed, I skipped without a scruple. If the characters talked quartet fashion, I lopped off the attributes. Proper names, which always gave me great trouble, I left unpronounced. Speeches in dialect, intrusions by the author, I ruthlessly excised. Reading only the dialogue, all that remained when I'd finished my abridgment, I found that I could follow the story line. More or less.

More difficult to justify was skipping of another sort. If, after a lengthy session at Baker Library, the ratio of pages completed to those still to go seemed insignificantly changed since the previous check, I slid deeper into the wingback chair, and, watching to be sure that neither Marie nor the librarian was looking, I turned over twenty, thirty, fifty pages, as many as I dared, in one lightning flip. This certainly was cheating at its most naked. I rationalized it by telling myself that no book should be 536 — *536!* — pages long.

"You *skipped!*" Marie would say in an Irish whisper if she caught me at it. She was as shocked as she would have been had I nudged a croquet ball into position.

Of course I paid for these great leaps forward. After each one, I found myself hopelessly out of touch with the story. Still, the out-of-touchness was a matter of degree, and on balance was worth it. At least at these times there was no mystery about why I was lost, as there frequently was at other times without any reason that I could see. Active skips, whether large or small, could be controlled by an act of will. I had only to force myself to read a description or resist the temptation to flip. Difficult words, proper names, sentences with structures insufficiently simple and declarative, these too I was aware of not even attempting. But what of the times when, as a result of a crisis of conscience over my heinous behavior, I thought I was doggedly reading every word, only to come to, like a patient suffering from amnesia, in unfamiliar terrain? While my eyes had been going through the motions of reading, my mind had been elsewhere. But where? The most I could have said was that it had been switched off.

What helped me finally to deal with these fugues was the very important and accidental discovery I made some years later (perhaps during my sophomore year in high school) that my mind was far from blank. It was busy with daydreams. Had Marie or one of my teachers accused me of daydreaming, I would have been indignant, for I was no more aware that I was planning the next day's picnic or whirling around as the queen of the Winter Carnival than are many people of their nighttime dream activity. (A skillful remedial therapist, who would have realized that I was rebelliously resisting the printed page while supposedly reading, would have helped me to draw these fantasies out of what seemed a blank, in the way that a psychotherapist encourages a patient to remember dreams. I would then have been able to do the same thing for myself, after which my attention would have been freed to focus on the page.)

What would snap me out of my reverie at Baker Library was a whispered "What's happening now?" from Marie, which brought my attention back to the page and made me realize that I was lost. At such moments I became frightened and was filled with the old feeling of helplessness: I was again the powerless victim of an incurable disease, and would never, never learn to read.

As might be expected, I was not the ideal companion "to discuss" *Little Women* with, but as Marie had no other on the walks home from the library along Tuck Drive and down School Street, she made do with me. Which sister would I like to be? she asked. With only a slippery grasp of the characters, it was difficult for me to say. I hedged. Marie wanted to be Jo. In a half-hearted way I did too, mainly because Jo's was a voice I could distinguish. She was also tomboyish and careless about her clothes, like me, but her bookishness, daring, and independence made her far more like Marie. So I claimed in these which-sister-would-you-like-to-be discussions that I wanted to be Beth. The goody-goody, the sickly, the not-very-bright Beth who, lucky girl, was "too bashful to go to school."

Marie's outrage at my skipping reached a climax the day it came out that, because of a whopping flip, I didn't know that

Beth had died. "How *could* you have missed it? It's one of the most important scenes in the book." No wonder I had remained unaccustomedly dry-eyed, one of the few girls my age to read *Little Women* without shedding a tear.

All through July and August, whenever it rained, I lugged the green book to Baker Library and took up the struggle. As September approached it became clear that there was no possibility of my finishing it. The vacation over, it was packed with my belongings, and eventually I misplaced it so efficiently that it was lost for good. For years I claimed to have read it. It was the one classic on readings lists I could talk about. I knew, now, that Beth had died and that one was supposed to have been heartbroken. I could express disappointment in Jo's marriage and, with genuine feeling, voice resentment toward the author for arranging it.

Although Louisa May Alcott had reinforced my aversion to the kind of books favored by teachers and librarians, and not for anything in the world would I have read *Jo's Boys* or any of the sequels, I had nevertheless read more words that summer than I had in fourth, fifth, and sixth grades put together, thanks to Marie's goading.

Goading was what I was aware of at the time. Now I see that what was crucial was her having read the opening pages to me. Without that leg-up no amount of goading would have got me going. Into the impenetrable rock that that massive book was to me, she had chiseled an opening. Intuitively, she had hit on what would have been the best method to educate me at that time. It was the pedagogical method W. B. Yeats's father adopted. When John Butler Yeats finally realized how useless it was to bully his son to read aloud, when his son was clearly incapable of doing so, the father took over the reading himself. From the time the boy was nine until he was sixteen, father read to son from Macaulay, Scott, Shakespeare, Shelley, Rossetti, Blake — the narrative verse and prose a poet would need to know when he began to write his own verses. Yeats's description is worth quoting:

> My father's influence upon my thoughts was at its height. We went to Dublin by train every morning, breakfasting in his studio. He had taken a large room with a beautiful eighteenth-century mantelpiece in a York Street tenement house, and at breakfast he read passages from the poets, and always from the play or poem at its most passionate moment.

John Butler Yeats selected the best writers, read aloud the most passionate moments, and continued to do so until his son was long past the age when most parents would have considered him too old to be read to.

In the biographies and autobiographies of famous people who were dyslexic, I have been struck by how often they had a parent who knew instinctively that this was the way to help the child who couldn't read to himself. Hans Christian Andersen's father read him Holberg's plays and the *Arabian Nights*. Thomas Edison, who says his father thought he was "stupid," was read Gibbon, Shakespeare, and Dickens by his mother. Woodrow Wilson, who didn't learn the alphabet until he was nine and couldn't read until he was eleven, was read to by his older sisters as well as by his parents.

Flaubert spent hours listening to a neighbor, "Uncle" Mignot, recite Cervantes. Without having read a word of *Don Quixote*, Flaubert came to know it by heart. (Young Gustave's way of putting an end to a family scene over his backwardness was to say, "Why bother to learn to read when 'Uncle' Mignot reads to me?" This was defensive of course. The neighbor performed an essential service not rendered by his parents.)

Marie, at thirteen, didn't have the confidence to continue reading to me. Had she read me all of *Little Women*, she

would have been told, wrongly, that she was babying me,
and that she risked killing any initiative I might have developed to read to myself.

On the overnight train back to New York, I carried another
book. Aunt Helen had just given it to me for my birthday.
My heart always sank when I was given a book as a gift, and
it sank when Aunt Helen suggested I take her gift to read on
the Pullman. The trip home was long. Marie, buried in her
book, was unreachable. The only resource I had against boredom and mounting apprehension about the coming year in a
new school was to count the telephone poles between stations — Bellows Falls, Brattleboro, Springfield — and hypno-
tize myself by staring at the converging and diverging wires.
After the train left Boston, the term ahead grew closer and
closer. The standards in the new school would be very high,
Miss Shapiro had said. When Marie saw that I was fretting,
she asked why I didn't look at Aunt Helen's gift. It was called
The Outdoor Girls at Deepdale. The dust jacket showed two
girls, about seventeen years old, dressed in white blouses and
long skirts. I looked to see how many pages there were. A
third as many as in *Little Women*. I could tell that this was
not the kind of book Miss Shapiro would have approved of.
Books in a series, like *The Rover Boys*, were not *real* books. I
noticed that the print was large; that meant it would go fast.
It opened with a sprightly dialogue. The girls were excited
about having lost something. What could it be?

After *Little Women*, *The Outdoor Girls at Deepdale* seemed
almost easy. It was all dialogue. I didn't finish it either, but I
read enough to be able to tell Marie the plot. By the time we
reached Grand Central I said, in what I hoped would pass for
literary conversation, that I was crazy about *The Outdoor
Girls* books. The next time I had to take an overnight train
ride, or was sick, I would read another in the series.

Chapter VI

From the beginning Orton's theory provoked wide-spread opposition among reading authorities in the education field, for it ran directly counter to two of the most powerful trends in progressive education at that time. The first of these was the whole-word method of teaching reading, which had in many cases supplanted the "obsolete" phonic method of teaching reading . . . The other trend was the wave of enthusiasm for interpreting all educational disabilities in psychiatric terms.

"The Last Skill Acquired," by Calvin Tomkins,
The New Yorker, September 13, 1963

The Model School of the New York Teachers' Training College, where my sister and I began classes in September, was surrounded by an extended campus, with City College on one side, Manhattanville College on the other, and opposite the Presbyterian Orphanage. The school building, with its well-lit, well-ventilated classrooms, amphitheater for demonstration lessons, kitchen for cooking instruction, and fully equipped gymnasium for physical training, was as up-to-date as were the school's textbooks, mimeographed sheets of unbound pages so new they were put into the students' hands when the ink was barely dry. On the faculty were women crammed with the latest pedagogical theories being expounded at nearby Columbia University. Classes were smaller than those in Inwood, allowing the teachers, assisted by seniors from the college who were doing their practice teaching, to give the students considerably more attention than they received in other city schools.

With Auntie, who was in the principal's office, we set out each morning for Convent Avenue and 135th Street. In her sensible clothes, made of serviceable materials in practical colors (which hid a coquettishness I only discovered much later), Auntie looked, as people used to say, as one would expect an auntie to look. Not necessarily ours, however. In body type we were so different, she short and stocky, the two of us tall and thin, that those who for some reason expected us to look like her children were struck by the almost comical difference between us. What had driven her coquettishness underground was a tendency to obesity that made clothes a problem. Sweets, for which she had a passion, were changed, almost instantly by her very efficient metabolic machinery, as she used to say, into fat. She never permitted herself to relax into a jolly fatness. Disliking her appearance, she waged a never-ending, if episodic, battle against weight. That Marie and I, who anatomically resembled our mother's family, remained slim no matter how much we ate was a cause of wonderment to her. It was the only way that she ever permitted herself to refer favorably to my appearance, fearful as she was that the comments of others would turn my head. "You're so *slim*," she'd say wistfully as the years went by and I still didn't put on weight. Then she'd add severely, "Are you sure you're eating properly?" Despite her weight and a penchant for carrying heavy packages, she had a lively, nimble gait. She was anxious about being late and was consequently always in a hurry. Chronophobia caused her to set clocks an hour ahead "to be on the safe side," with the result that she, and now we, arrived at the Model School an hour before the first bell.

Before and after the vacation when, from time to time, I'd expressed concern about the change of school, Auntie had assured me that with an academic history such as mine a shift in milieu would be all to the good. The new teachers, having no preconceptions about my ability, would allow me to make a fresh start. She had prepared them for my academic difficulties by painting an amusing and touching picture of the Whirligig period, blaming my illiteracy on antiquated textbooks and outmoded teaching methods. Shrewdly, she put me over to them as "a challenge," knowing well that nothing stimulated the Model School teachers so much as a challenge.

How to deal with the surfeit of attention that came to me as a result of being a challenge was my major concern during the early weeks in the new school. A criminal tracked by a searchlight would have been no more on the spot than I was.

My head ached from the bright light that relentlessly shone on me. Another worry was that part of the attention came to me because I was a relative of Auntie's. I was as eager as ever to be a favorite, but I had no wish to be a fake favorite because of Auntie's friendships with my teachers. Above all, I was afraid it would alienate my classmates. They might clamor around me in the school yard jeering "Teacher's Pet," the way they did to another girl in my class whose older sister was on the faculty of the training college.

On this score I need not have been concerned. Far from being envious, my classmates pitied me. As well they might, for what had occurred in class, good or bad, had been reported to Auntie by the time I went down to her office at the end of the day. As I helped her to finish her work by feeding the insatiable mimeograph machine, I heard over the slap-slapslap of the freshly inked pages (addenda to update the up-to-date texts) a rundown on my quotidian failures. It was I, cranking the machine, who had envious daydreams. If only I were an orphan without relatives, like the Presbyterian students who lived across the street! Theirs was not a bad lot, it seemed to me. From careful questioning I had discovered that the orphans were looked after by parent substitutes who were too busy to give them more than custodial attention. Mr. and Mrs. Johnson, the directors of the Presbyterian Orphanage, whom I had a chance to observe when they came to visit during Open School Week, were bland and benign. Mr. Johnson smiled nervously all the time, and Mrs. Johnson seemed to have all she could do to control the wisps of hair that floated free from her bun.

When I questioned the orphans about what the Johnsons were like, they said with a shrug, "They're OK." The insouciance of this response made me suspect that the Johnsons were ideal guardians. What I would have liked best about institutional life was that little attention was paid to report cards. There were too many of them. The directors had time only to sign them and say, "Try to do better next time." If I were an orphaned-orphan . . .

But I was not. There was Auntie, and Auntie had no intention of giving up on me. She had told my new teachers that contrary to the evidence I presented I was not stupid. They tended to believe her, for I didn't look dull-witted, and tried to think of ways to help me. Unfortunately, up-to-date as they were, they had not heard of Orton, who was at that time working close by at the Neurological Institute of Columbia Presbyterian Medical Center. Nor had they heard of Anna Gillingham who, not far from Convent Avenue, at the Ethical Culture School, was experimenting with remedial techniques. These techniques she perfected when she joined Orton's staff. With Bessie W. Stillman she wrote, some years later, what became the classic instruction manual, *Remedial Reading.*

The Gillingham-Stillman system, and the many variations on it developed since, recognizes that what dyslexics need is not to have more of the same kind of training — be it the "whole-word" method, which came into fashion in the mid-twenties, or a combination of new and old, "whole-word" and phonetics — that children have in the classroom. Dyslexics need different training. For them each stage in the process of learning to read must be broken down into many small steps: each step taught slowly and thoroughly, the learning reinforced by engaging as many sense organs as possible — ear, eye, touch, and with it the musculature of the fingers and arms — in what is called tri-modal reinforcement.

Instead of having had me read aloud the same passage in a story until I made no errors, a remedial teacher would have recognized that I needed to begin at the beginning, with the alphabet. Using objects — an apple, a bottle, a china cat — I would have been taught to associate *a* with apple, *b* with bottle, *c* with cat, all the way to *z* with a glass zebra. I would have held the objects, heard the teacher say the *a*, heard and felt my speech organs repeat it after her. I would have written the *a*, learning the feel of it with my fingers and arms, would have traced a cut-out *a*, or an *a* made in sandpaper. I would also have drawn an apple. The teacher's attentiveness would have kept a pupil like me, who had the attention span of a six-year-old for this kind of lesson, from associating the stick of gum with the letter *j*, or the jack with the letter *g*. At no time would I have been permitted to guess — or, more important, to make an error, for what is learned incorrectly must be relearned. Careful structuring of the material presented would have guaranteed me success. Even a limited success, such as this, would have begun the difficult process of rebuilding my self-confidence and overcoming my resistance to the written word.

Because no two dyslexics are alike, the symptoms and degree of severity differing widely among them, remediation must be tailored to suit individual needs. I had two strengths many dylexics lack. I was not hyperactive, and my writing was legible and produced without effort. Had my letters been difficult to read, or produced laboriously (dysgraphia), I would have had to be retrained, through finger and arm exercises, before being allowed to go on to cursive letter forms and connectives.

By the time I entered the Model School I would have learned to associate objects with letters very quickly (far more quickly than I would have at the time I entered Miss Henderson's class). But to be certain that I had the alphabet down pat, my teacher would have tested to see whether I knew the letters out of sequence. Did I know what letter preceded and followed *m*? Not without running from *a* to *b* to *c* all the way to *m*. There would have been more drill in the alphabet then, called overteaching, before we moved to the next step: phonetics.

Beginning with the short vowel, the *a* in apple again, I would have learned the *a* in "at," "bat," "cat," "fat," "had." Then the same *a* in two-syllable words: "ambush," "cabin," "combat." So with the *i*. Having learned *a* and *i*, I would have been taught to distinguish the way "pat" and "pit," "pan" and "pin" sound and are written. No difficulty here? Then on to the next step, and the next. At the lesson for the final *e*, we would have come to a dead stop. Since I had no idea how the final *e* affects the sound of a word, I added it haphazardly to any word that I thought had an unfinished look. No more of that. I would have been trained to hear the difference between "pin" and "pine," so that I would have understood that the final *e* is not decorative; it serves a purpose. "Mat," "mate"; "hat," "hate." Drill, drill, drill.

Following this step-by-step progression, moving from one- to two- to three-syllable words, from simple letter-sound patterns to the more complex blending of vowels and consonants, I would have learned to decode: to read. Encoding, putting thoughts into written words, is learned along with decoding. In preparation for being asked to write on "What I Like Best About Summer," a favorite post-vacation English assignment that made my head feel as if it were filling with hot air, I would have been taught first to write a sentence, dictating one to the teacher, having her dictate it back to me. Then a paragraph. Before tackling a book report on *Heidi*, I would have been given a short text, perhaps a newspaper article in which the language was at a level I could understand, and been taught to find out what the author was saying, what characters or incidents he was describing, and would have been asked to write about them with the help of a word guide to insure that the spelling would be correct.

No matter how much training I had had in spelling I, like most dyslexics, would probably never have become a good speller. As Orton said, and remedial teachers have since confirmed, poor spelling cannot be cured. It can be improved, however, vastly improved, by thorough training in phonetics and the learning of spelling rules, like the very useful "*i* before *e*."

Since spelling and intelligence are so inextricably linked in the minds of the educated public that they use a person's spelling as a rough-and-ready test of his intelligence (a linkage no efforts by psychologists are likely to break), the importance of teaching spelling cannot be overestimated. Dyslexics resist writing because they are reluctant to project an image of themselves which they feel does not do their intelligence justice. Also, they are aware that nothing is easier to ridicule than incorrect spelling.

Knowing how little chance I had of writing, without error, the kind of thank-you note that would have expressed my genuine feelings about a gift, I resorted to a safe (or almost safe) and wooden formula:

> Deare Aunt or Uncle So and So,
>
>   Thank you for the _____. It is just what I wanted. I hope you and Aunt (or Uncle So and So) are well. Marie and I are both fine.
>
>   Your loving ("i before e," etc.)
>   niece,

Even so, rarely did my note pass the censor. As often as not, Auntie returned it with the "dear" or some other word corrected, and the instruction to rewrite it before it was sent out. Had I learned the rule that in words with *ea*, the silent *a* usually signals that the *e* is long, I would have known that there is no need for a final *e* on "dear" and would not have wasted time speculating about whether to put it on or leave it off.

Instead of coming to a dead stop every time I had to add a verb suffix, such as -*ing* or -*ed*, to a word, I would have learned to apply the 1-1-1 rule: if in a word there is one syllable, one (and only one) vowel, and one consonant after the vowel, one doubles the last consonant before adding the suffix. So "swim" becomes "swimming"; "rub" — "rubbing"; "shop" — "shopping." On the other hand, the final consonant is not doubled in "stand" and "crash" because, having two consonants after the vowel, these words are not governed by the 1-1-1 rule.

While no amount of looking at, or writing, the word "swimming" would have taught me to spell it correctly, and not "swiming" or "swimiming," I could have remembered the rule. A few lessons to learn it, repeated drill to reinforce it, and I would have had it firmly in my head for ready reference.

For want of such training and the learning of such rules, I might have been in danger of failing at the Model School (where the "whole-word" method was used to teach reading), had not the teachers there taken up the challenge of educating me in a new way. They, who had not heard of Orton, had heard the fashionable theory then in the air that students who were obviously bright but yet had difficulty learning to read were "blocked" emotionally. Rather than drill me in the basic skills, they would unblock me. How? By "bringing out" my imagination. Did I have talent for art? For crafts? For making up stories? The art teacher, the crafts teacher, the English teacher tried to coax out my ability.

During the months they tried out this theory, I spoiled reams of drawing paper, ruined linoleum blocks, bruised my thumb with the hammer, drew blood with the needle, was dumb during storytelling time. It was not a question of overcoming timidity, I tried to tell them. There was *nothing there*. Only after months of frustration and failure did they abandon their unblocking experiment. The relief I felt as one teacher after the other lost hope and gave up on me was quickly followed by apprehension. Did this mean that they'd decided that I *was* stupid? Or emotionally disturbed? And if so, what would they do with me? Would I be put into an ungraded class in another school? Or perhaps even sent away to a special school?

My home-room teacher, Miss O'Connor, who had been less enthusiastic about the fashionable theory and the search for talent than the others, wanted me to know at the beginning of the second quarter that she was not discouraged. She would try a different approach, she said. She would "work around the problem." In subjects in which I did poorly — reading, spelling, arithmetic, whatever required the printed word, the "old" subjects and formerly the important ones — she ignored my failures. In the "new" subjects — history, geography, civics — she did what she could do to stimulate me.

It was during the teaching of the new subjects that the climate in the classroom differed so markedly from any I had known before. At P.S. 52 to be good had meant to sit up straight and maintain an attitude of passive attentiveness: both easy for me. At the Model School, while one was not permitted to leave one's seat and wander around (as rumor had it was permitted at *really* progressive schools), the great thing was to be active, "to participate." If I wanted to be good now, and I wanted to more than ever because of the reports that were telegraphed to Auntie's office, I saw that I would have to be lively. I would have "to participate." And — this was essential — I would have to ask "intelligent questions."

Miss O'Connor's yearning for these questions was so palpable that when she trained the bright light in my eye and pleaded, "Don't *you* have a question you'd like to ask?" I longed to gratify her. It wasn't easy. After years of trying to attract as little attention to my intellectual performance as possible, after years of suppressing all questions that came to mind because I suspected that I was the only student in the class not to know the answer, I had no muscles in my brain for the new sport.

In the beginning, when Miss O'Connor tried to draw me out, I tightened my lips and shook my head. I could think of nothing but the high buzz in my ears, and wished only to be ignored. The children around me, who'd had years of this sort of thing, were so eager to participate that they strained out of their seats and waved their hands in frantic eagerness to contribute.

After a while the arm waving, the straining, the enthusiasm made me ache to join in the play. I liked Miss O'Connor, was grateful for her eagerness to help me. She was asking so little; couldn't I comply? In the subway, doing my homework, before going to sleep at night, I racked my brains looking for questions. Finally nature came to my aid. One morning when we left Inwood, Auntie insisted we wear rubbers, loathsome rubbers, because it was raining. When we emerged from the subway at 135th Street the sidewalks were dry. How come it was raining uptown and not here? I wondered as I trudged along in the heavy and now unnecessary overshoes.

How come? Wasn't that a question? When, during the geography lesson the class was discussing rainfall, my arm shot up with the others, Miss O'Connor's face creased in a beatific smile. It wasn't the quality of the question that mattered, or even its relevancy; it was enough that I was participating. At the end of the day, when I went to Auntie's office, I could tell by her mood that a communiqué had reached her with good news: I had caught the school spirit. I was taking hold.

Answers, not surprisingly, came harder than questions, but in the excitement of group participation, I even found some of these. More important, as a result of the we're-working-on-this-problem-as-a-team attitude I forgot to worry about being stupid and lost the self-consciousness which had previously inhibited me in areas where I might have been able to function. The thrill I'd felt during the oral arithmetic test in Miss Shapiro's class, when I had felt my brain work as clearly as at other times I'd felt my heart beat, began to be repeated more and more frequently. I hugged these moments of illumination. For the first time I stopped dragging my feet on the way to school. The old subjects continued to suck me back into lethargy, but thanks to the modified departmental system followed at the Model School, it was never for long. Bells summoned us to the amphitheater for a demonstration lesson, which was almost as exciting as being in a play, or to the kitchen to learn to make goldenrod eggs, or to the gymnasium where, after I shot three baskets in a row, my teammates elected me captain.

During that Christmas vacation, which Marie and I spent as we did many vacations with our mother's relatives in Westchester, I made an astonishing discovery: My mother had also had difficulty learning to read. Uncle Charlie knew, of course, about my problem. Had Auntie not told him, he would have caught on quickly enough on those evenings when, after dinner, he played the piano and Marie and I sang songs from musical comedies or arias from Italian opera. The melodies I learned quickly enough and sang in a strong alto, but the words . . . the words came out a jumble. "Ramona, we'll meet beside the waterfall" was no easier for me than "Questa o quella per me pari sono a quant'altre d'intorno." I guessed, I invented, I faked my way along, doing a good deal of "la-la-la-ing" to keep up with the accompanist.

Uncle Charlie pretended he didn't notice. If he sensed that I was embarrassed about a mistake I'd made, he'd say, "I must get your Uncle Matthew's old violin down from the attic. With your left-handedness you'll learn to play it quickly." And to Aunt Hilda, he'd say, "I think she has a talent for music." He never looked for the violin, and I understood that what he was saying was: Never mind about not being able to read; you'll find something else you'll be good at. I didn't share his optimism, but his reassurance, like my grandmother's, refreshed my spirit and helped me to believe, at least for the moment, that somehow I'd be able to muddle through life despite my limitations.

It was after one of these post-prandial sings that Aunt Hilda, reminiscing about my mother and her sister, remarked casually that "the girls," as she called them, had been in the same grade in school. Since my mother was the elder by a year, I wondered: how come? I thought about it before going to sleep that night and the next day I questioned Aunt Hilda. She said she didn't know. Wasn't it that our grandmother had thought that since the girls were so close it would be nice for them to be in class together?

Knowing how Marie would have hated such an arrangement, close as we were, I asked if my mother hadn't protested. Aunt Hilda's vagueness aroused my suspicion. My grandmother, when I brought it up with her, was at first equally vague. In time I pieced together what I think was the explanation. The nuns who taught "the girls" must have advised Grandmother to let my mother repeat a year, probably the third grade, so that she could be with a younger reading group. St. Lawrence's Academy on Park Avenue was a genteel school, run in a genteel fashion. No ugly threats of being left back would have been made. (It may even have been arranged so smoothly that my mother wasn't humiliated.) My grandmother, who was not intellectually ambitious for her daughters, acquiesced, and gave out as the reason for the demotion the one Aunt Hilda had given me.

Only in the most nebulous way did I understand at the time that my mother was the genetic link to my dyslexia. What I had learned by accidentally uncovering the family skeleton was that my disability was not unique. My mother had had it. And somehow she had got through school. I knew from the contents of her velvet jewelry box that she had received a gold medal for excellence at graduation, knew also that to pass the time in the acceptable way before marriage, she had taught for a year or two in the Academy's lower school. It was this knowledge, I think now, that allowed Grandmother to be so little concerned about me. My mother had learned to read eventually, and so would I. What was all the fuss about?

Was my grandmother also dyslexic? I had no evidence that she was. From whom my mother's inheritance came, I don't know. Had I had children there is a good chance that one of them would have inherited the disability from me. None of Marie's children was dyslexic but two of her grandsons are, one to the same degree I am, and with identical symptoms. (His early history in no way resembles mine; he was as healthy as I was sickly, and was raised at home by both parents.)

After Christmas vacation I returned to the Model School with the gift my Westchester relatives had unknowingly given me. If there were no other children in my class like me, I nonetheless felt less freakish than I had before because of what I'd learned about my mother. I also found the second term to be easier in every way than the first had been. My teachers were now confident they could help me, and I knew what it was to have small but daily successes. At the end of the year for the first time it was not inconceivable to me that I should be promoted, this time not because I was a goody-goody, or was tall for my age, or even because I was Auntie's niece, but because I'd learned a reasonable percentage of what was in the seventh grade syllabus. At least in the new subjects.

Had my school life not taken this fortuitous turn, I might well have felt lost when, the following year, my sister went to high school and, for the first time, we were separated. But in eighth grade, when I ceased to be quite so challenging a challenge and when, through clowning and success on the basketball court, I became a personality in my own right rather than a relative of Auntie's, I began to enjoy being me. Miss O'Meara, following Miss O'Connor's lead, played down my failures and built up my successes. I was full of questions, agitated my hand to be called on, and spoke with growing self-confidence about rearmament, which I was dead against, and Gandhi, whom I'd just heard of and was all for.

In the school yard, when such matters were discussed, I found that I could join in conversations about "being good in" or "being bad in" this or that subject; it was no longer an undifferentiated mass of failures. I was good in civics, history, and geography, good in oral arithmetic, bad in written arithmetic, terrible in spelling. As for reading, the less said about it the better. Where I was bad, I was very, very bad, but as no one asked me to read aloud anymore, nor held up to ridicule my bizarre spelling, my classmates were none the wiser.

The lunchroom talk about high schools, which became obsessive during the last semester, jolted me out of this period of relative complacency.

"Whatschooleryougointo?" one girl would ask another.

"Me? Julia Richmond."

"Whyyagoin *there?* It's all girls."

"Yeah. I know. My father, he's old fashion, he doesn't want me with boys. Too much foolinaround and no studying, he says." And to me, "Whereyougoin?"

"George Washington," I'd say. George Washington, the golden cupola shining on the hill above Inwood, the scene of decorated gymnasiums, proms, and romance.

"Luck-kee," would say my envious friend who was going to an all-girls' school. "What course? Academic or commercial?"

"Academic," I'd say, as casually as I knew how. From Marie and her friends at George Washington, I had heard that to be in the commercial course was to be buried alive.

One wouldn't stand a chance of being elected captain of the basketball team, and of course, college would be out.

"Academic? Gee, that's hard."

If it was hard, how would I get into it? And suppose I did? How long would it take the high school teachers to catch on that, thanks to my training at the Model School, I talked smarter than I was?

Much depended on the placement tests. Yet there was no way to prepare for them. Yes, there was, said Auntie: review. Review? I knew how to review orally, with the teacher's guidance. What to do on my own? Auntie pressed a bundle of mimeographed pages into my hands. Without the stimulation of the class, I was lost. It was not now a question of listening attentively. It was up to me to read the text. But reading was still such *an effort*, tiring me in a way no other activity did. As I tried to study, my eyes began to scud down the page, unable to hang on to the words. Before long my eyelids drooped, my frame slackened, my head swung down to my chest. I was asleep.

The day of the test I went to George Washington with the other elementary school students who were applying for admission. We were directed to a room and handed test booklets by a proctor. At the signal we were to open them: Go! At the top of the first page was a long, dense paragraph of instructions. Instructions had always caused me particular trouble. So much was said in so few words that what was intended was rarely clear. If Auntie said, as she often did apropos of some household chore, "Read the directions," I balked, seeing it as another version of the "sign-game," another way to trick me into reading. Now I was on my own with instructions I had to understand if I was to pass the test. I recognized most of the words, but what did they say *to do?* I looked at the others around me. They were working rapidly, doing what they had been instructed to do. The proctor

looked at me meaningfully: no cheating. Too weak to protest, I turned back to my booklet. My hands made wet marks
on the paper. My fingers cramped around the pencil. *I must
not get panicky*, I told myself in panic. I knew what the words
meant. I had only to string them together. And to think. How
could I think when my brain had turned to ice? How it
ached!

The proctor rang a warning bell. Just five minutes left.
Giddy now, I raced from page to page, guessing at the questions by their shapes. This one must require underlining, this
one inserting, or deleting, or correcting. Another booklet: the
arithmetic test. "If a shopkeeper has seven bolts of cloth
. . ." The sentence went on so long that by the time I
reached the period I had forgotten the question in the subordinate clause. Slowly, slowly. If a shopkeeper has how many
bolts of cloth?

Afterward, on the way home, my friends and I held a post
mortem:

"What did they want us to do in that last question?"

"What did you get for the one about the postage stamps?"

"I thought it was a cinch."

"I thought it was really hard."

"I thought it was unfair."

Sick at heart, I remained silent. Four dreary years of
studying shorthand, typing, and bookkeeping, at which I suspected I would do even less well than at Latin and geometry,
loomed ahead. I would not be elected to the prom committee
and as for being invited to the Winter Carnival . . .

Fortunately the admissions office paid less attention to the
test results than to a letter from the principal of the Model
School. Dr. Walsh wrote that I had made "great strides" during the last two years. My teachers felt that my "potential"
was considerably higher than was shown by my scores. All
things considered, I belonged in the academic program.

Graduation day, wearing a dress of white paper taffeta, I

received the embraces of my relatives, the good wishes of my teachers, an award for excellence in athletics, and a parchment diploma to which was affixed a red ribbon and a gold seal. Instead of being shunted into the commercial course, I was going into the academic program at the high school of my dreams. Who said miracles didn't happen?

Chapter VII

The difficulty in consulting dictionaries etc., is probably typical. I cannot glance down a page and pick
out a word I'm looking for, but have to scrutinize
every word . . .

> From an autobiographical fragment written
> by a retired lawyer, a dyslexic, in
> *Reading Disability*, by Knud Hermann

The phenomenon of "passing" . . . has a high price
in anxiety, for these people live in a world that
teeters on the verge of collapse at any moment. They
are constantly liable to being exposed and therefore
to being discredited.

> "Psychiatric Aspects of Dyslexia,"
> by Dr. Howard D. Rome, *Bulletin
> of The Orton Society*, XXI, 1971

Freshmen who lived in Inwood were not permitted to approach George Washington High School directly by way of the road that led from Dyckman Street up to Fort George. Like heroes in medieval tales, they were put to many tests before being allowed to pass through the august portals of the (always capitalized) Main Building. They were made to cool their heels for a year, sometimes two, in an antechamber or annex.

The annex to which I was assigned, one of three necessary to house the 800 entering students, was a grubby, overcrowded building two blocks north of Academy Street where we lived. From having been twenty in a class at the Model School, we were now never fewer than forty. Arm-breaking loads of books, most of them in terminal condition, were issued to us the first day. Assignments were written on the blackboard at the beginning of each period. The following day one handed in written work or not; was graded accordingly. One was called on to recite. One responded or not; was graded accordingly. Absences, lateness, inattentiveness, disruptive behavior were noted, together with grades, on a small white card in the teacher's desk book. At the marking period, warning notes were sent home. One was no longer a child, one was told; the days of spoon-feeding were over.

Happy to have climbed another step on the ladder to adulthood (to be addressed as "Miss" instead of by my given name) and eager to head off warning notes addressed to Auntie, I vowed to be conscientious. The great thing, I knew, was not to fall behind. Each day at noon, when those of us in the morning session were dismissed, instead of staying in the school yard to play basketball, I went straight home to study.

In our house Latin had considerable prestige. There was to be no nonsense, Auntie said, about substituting Spanish (considered the easy way out for students who weren't serious). Without Latin one was not educated. My father and his brothers, who had received a classical education in Jesuit schools, had been sufficiently fluent in Latin to carry on a conversation when they wished not to be understood by others. This would have seemed to me, as I prepared the assigned passage in *The Argonauts*, one of Auntie's exaggerations had I not the previous summer come upon a notebook of my father's in the attic of the Long Island cottage, in which was a group of poems he had written in Latin. If I studied my conjugations and declensions, one day I might be able to find out what the poems were about, and why he had chosen not to write them in English.

It was the fashion to groan about how difficult Latin was, so I groaned publicly, but the truth was that in many ways Latin was easier for me than English. It was logical. It was pronounced phonetically. It was spelled predictably. I was beginning at the beginning, learning a few words at a time, instead of coming in late as I had done with English. And since everyone in the class had to go slowly in reading it aloud, even here I was at no great disadvantage.

In algebra, occasions for reversing digits, especially when using logarithm tables, were numerous. Not realizing wherein my errors lay, I made a heightened effort not to be "careless." History, for the student who was willing to be attentive in class, especially one who was having her first male teacher, was easier than the other subjects. Easier by far than English. The novel assigned for the semester looked unpromising, but with my new determination, I would not be put off by such superficial things as a drab binding. I opened and read:

> A Saturday afternoon in November was approaching the time of twilight. And the last tract of unenclosed wild known as Egdon Heath embrowned itself moment by moment. Overhead the hollow stretch of whitish cloud shutting out the sky was a tent which had the whole heath for a floor.

Ugh! I skipped to the next chapter to see if it was any better.

> Along the road walked an old man. He was white-haired as a mountain, bowed in the shoulders and faded in general aspect.

Embrowned in gloom, bowed in shoulders, I was well on my way to developing an aversion to Hardy that would not easily be overcome.

By midterm there seemed no way to avoid a warning in English. About the other subjects, I felt a guarded optimism — an optimism that was shattered the morning I awakened with a raging fever and the all-too-familiar symptoms of flu. Oh, this treacherous body I had to drag around! How could it do this to me?

When I recovered, I found myself so far behind my classes there seemed no possibility of catching up. So many Latin vocabulary words to learn! So many algebra problems to solve! So many book reports to hand in! Attentiveness in class, intelligent questions, intuitive leaps and guesswork, on which I had learned to depend, would not get me out of this jam.

If I failed this semester, it would mean that I'd become a "repeater." I'd be like the oafish boys who sat in the back of the room, making obscene jokes and otherwise causing trouble, waiting for the day when they could drop out of school and join the ranks of the unemployed. They didn't seem to worry about how they would earn a living. I did. Auntie frequently reminded Marie and me that the money our father had left us would run out by the time we were twenty-one. We would then have to be self-supporting. With the specter of unemployment all around us, I worried that it might be difficult for one not richly endowed with intelligence or talent to find a job. Outside the Dyckman Street subway station a man sat behind an up-ended crate, selling apples. Or rather, trying to sell them. Never, in the many times I passed him, did I see him make a sale. He had dropped out of school, Auntie said. The victim of insufficient education, he would spend the rest of his days waiting for a buyer. At night I woke up in a cold sweat. In a repetitive dream I had, I was trying to earn a living selling apples.

My school-yard basketball-playing pals showed me a way out of my dilemma. Who needed to know the vocabulary to do a translation? one of them said when I complained that I couldn't play on Saturday because I was so far behind in my work. He flashed before my eyes a well-thumbed page torn from a book. It was the passage in *The Argonauts*, assigned for the following Monday, translated into English. Sure I could look at it, he said. If I got to the school yard early the next day, I could copy it before class. There was an even better aid, a line-by-line translation called a "trot." Naturally, it was harder to get hold of, especially before midterms and finals. It was said that one could sometimes, reading ahead in it, hit the passage that would be on the examination. And wait . . . there was more help. Book reports? A veritable circulating library of them had been bequeathed by last year's freshmen. A word changed here or there, rewritten neatly in one's own handwriting, and half the English problem was solved.

Down the greasy pole to the underworld I slid to a new life of crime, of cribbing, cheating, stealing. Whereas in the days when I manipulated the grocery money to buy cookies I had been a solitary operator, alone with my guilt, at the annex I had the support of organized crime. There was even the comforting myth that we were playing a game. It was a sport, as the jaunty words "trot" and "pony" suggested, to be played with daring and flare.

Of course there were terrible moments of panic. Would one's connection arrive with the book report on time? Had he overslept? Was he playing hooky? Was this the right meeting place? One raced up and down stairwells during the change of class to alternate meeting places. No one there? Alarm — followed by resignation. One simply had to borrow the book from someone who had read it, sniff it, palpate it, question the conscientious reader as skillfully as possible, and, if worst came to worst, read a little in it oneself. Or, if this was not possible, one had simply to bluff it out with the teacher: One had written the report but left it at home. The following day *without fail* one would bring it in — thereby gaining time to make another connection.

The greatest daring was required during examinations. The timid merely craned their necks to look at their neighbor's paper when the teacher's back was turned. The bold, of whom I was not one, consulted books hidden in their desks, read from notes inked on arms or hidden in stockings just above the knee, or, with nerves of iron, tiptoed down to look at the paper of the brightest boy in the class, who might or might not cup his hand prissily around his answers. Our teachers showed a surprising tolerance for the shuffling and whispering that went on, probably because with forty in the room it was not easy to maintain order. Only when the hum of activity reached a pitch they could no longer ignore, did they wheel around and shout, *"No cheating."*

Members of the underground held in contempt students who excelled. They were called "grinds," even "greasy-grinds." The pretense necessary to give the delinquents a feeling of superiority was that academic success came only to those who were willing to sacrifice everything to study. That "grinds," or "brains" as they were more politely labeled, were brighter or more gifted must on no account be admitted. I was unable to join my partners in crime in any enthusiastic disparagement of the stars in our class because I secretly admired them. Besides I was closely related to a brain. My sister, a sophomore up at the Main Building, was translating Caesar so elegantly that she was well on her way to winning the coveted Latin prize.

In my post-flu crisis, I had appealed to Marie for help. If she would just begin the translation for me, so that I knew what it was about . . . Marie helped me until the day Auntie pointed out to her that she was in effect doing my homework for me. More serious still, she was encouraging me to be dependent upon her and giving me a false sense of security. Afterward Marie refused her assistance unless I knew all the vocabulary, had made a conscientious effort on my own, and then had got stuck.

Look up *all those words?* That required running through the alphabet, forgetting where I was, beginning again, running through the alphabet, forgetting where I was . . . It took *time*. If I did that I would never get through my homework. Didn't Marie care that I was likely to become a repeater? Every evening there was a scene between us. I nagged, pleaded, whined, wept. My sister stood firm.

This running argument, the most painful and extended we'd ever had, was broken off abruptly the day I came home from school to find that Marie had been rushed to the hospital. Auntie, who vacillated between wanting to break my dependence on my sister, and being afraid of what would happen to me if she did, told me over the phone when she called to say Marie was going into the operating room, that there was nothing to worry about.

Why couldn't I see Marie? Could hospitals refuse a sister, even one under age, visiting rights? When I was finally allowed in, I found Marie reassuringly alive, but pale, and with a giant bandage where her appendix had been. I was permitted to visit her only once more before she was whisked off to convalesce at Aunt Hilda and Uncle Charlie's house in Westchester.

When friends called to ask after Marie, I was surprised to hear Auntie say that she was recovering nicely, but that I was not at all myself. It was true that the room Marie and I shared seemed too large, that the other bed was spookily empty, that there was never anyone to talk to when I came home from school, that I couldn't think of anything to say in my rudimentary letters to Marie, that her letters to me reported events taking place on another planet. Was this the same as missing her? Wasn't it an exaggeration to say that I was "wandering around like a lost soul"? I must learn to stand on my own two feet, Auntie said. If I didn't become more independent and develop inner resources, what would happen to me when Marie married and she and I began to lead separate lives?

Marie married? Separate lives? What was Auntie talking about? I wondered, not guessing that suburban social life in Westchester, which led to a precocity unknown among our age group in Inwood, had catapulted Marie into full-blown adolescence, causing her impatience to be grown up to accelerate at a faster rate than mine. She was learning to play bridge, while I was still playing Parcheesi. She was picking up a new vocabulary with words like "bored" and "weird"; I still spoke the Academy Street demotic. Now that she was up and about, with no classes to attend and time to kill, she was puffing on cigarettes, wearing lipstick, and arranging her hair in a way to make her look older than fifteen.

Little suspecting that in just three years Marie would be married and the separate lives Auntie threatened me with would begin, I worried not about what was going on in Westchester but about a new jam I was in at school. In the club I had joined, as part of the extracurricular activities my student advisor had hinted might make up for my academic deficiencies, the Newman Club, the young curate assigned to be its moderator had asked me to prepare "a little speech," to give before the group, on the clergyman for whom the club was named, John Henry Newman. It would mean going to the library and looking him up in a book . . .

Me prepare a speech? Father Ryan must have me mixed up with someone else (my sister perhaps?). Since I continued to associate standing before a group with punishment and humiliation — I could still hear Miss Henderson: "Come up here. Come right up here and read to the class" — I fell back into the old head-hanging, blushing, and mutism when called upon to do so. And as for looking up anything in the library . . . Was it too late to get out of the club? I wondered. It had been the advisor's bright idea, not mine. To have only sports on my list of activities would not make for a well-rounded extracurricular program, she'd said. What were my hobbies?

Dancing.

Dancing wasn't a hobby, she said scornfully. What about stamp collecting?

I loosened my jaw, rolled my eyes back in my head.

Or photography?

I didn't have a Brownie.

What religion was I? Catholic? Well then . . . She wrote Newman Club on my card and told me to report for the first meeting on Friday during lunch hour.

Clubs were supposed to be fun, weren't they? I said confronting her, after Father Ryan had approached me about the little speech. They were optional, weren't they? Not really it seemed. To drop out would show a deplorable lack of school spirit. I was trapped. Since there was no way out, the following Friday I would simply have to confess my limitations to Father Ryan. He had taken me for a bright student, when the truth was I had never been good in school, I'd always had trouble reading, and, as was well known to everyone but him, I was incapable of making a speech.

The mild-mannered curate, who turned out to be surprisingly obdurate, pretended this was self-deprecation. He had observed me with my friends, entertaining them (i.e., clowning). Had seen that I was articulate. Certainly not timid or shy.

In front of a group . . .

What better way to overcome that feeling than to speak before a small group of my peers? To help me get started, he would lend me a book of his own about Cardinal Newman, and would write down the name of a reference book I should consult in the library. Easy as pie.

If Marie had come to the library with me she would have at least told me where to find the book, even if she was being mean and wouldn't write my speech for me. But Marie hadn't come to the library. She was up in Westchester, smoking like a chimney. Which meant that I was at the mercy of my old adversary, the librarian with the dyed black hair.

"What?" the librarian said. "You mean to say you don't know where the *Encyclopaedia Britannica* is? *At your age?* You should be ashamed of yourself." She was paying me back for all those Saturdays when I hadn't checked out the books she'd recommended.

The set was over on the bottom shelf. She wasn't going to find the volume for me. I would have to look it up myself.

The phrase "look it up" was like a flying tile, hitting my temple a stunning blow. All mental activity came to a halt. This is what the word "stupid" meant: not to know how to look something up. I sat on a little stool facing the bottom row of books. I was a child again, a stupid little girl, sitting on a little stool. Overwhelmed with impotence and self-pity, I felt a giant ball of stone form in my throat. After a while I began to coax myself into activity: You can't sit here all day. Come on, try to think what to do. Looking something up is like looking up a word in the dictionary. You simply have to

look at the letters on the back of each volume until you come
to the right one.

Ideally one should be interested in the subject one looked
up. I didn't give a hoot about the dumb old club I'd been
bullied into joining, nor was I interested in the Cardinal.

"Maximilian — Naples" — here it was. Again the need to
run through the alphabet, *k, l, m, n*. How tiresome it grew!
And, just as I'd suspected, Newman wasn't there! That was
always the way. When you looked things up, they were never
where they were supposed to be. I took the volume over to
the librarian to show her that the *Encyclopaedia Britannica*
was not so encyclopedic after all.

Newman was there all right, she said, taking me rudely by
the ear. *If* you knew how to look him up. Only a Dumb Dora
would look for *New* in a volume that ended with *Nap*.

The humiliated child slunk back to the little stool. What
had the librarian meant? What had I done wrong? Since she
hadn't explained my mistake, I didn't know how to correct
it. (I had read *Nap* as *Npa*.) There was nothing to do but go
through the alphabet again . . . Na, nb, nc, nd, ne, nea, neb,
nec . . . new . . . Yes, there it was: Newman, John Henry,
1801–1890. There was a picture of a hollow-cheeked man in
clerical collar. From reading the text I would never find out
about him. It was just a lot of words that said nothing. It was
worse even than *The Return of the Native*.

The day I was to give the speech, I woke up before the
alarm, feeling decidedly ill. For once I didn't mind. My body
would have been hospitable to any virus. Unfortunately the
thermometer did not register a fever. No, I could not stay
home, said Auntie. As the day went on I'd probably feel better. I knew that was unlikely. All morning, during classes, the
thought of the noon-hour club meeting made me feel seasick.
When time for it came, I made one more attempt to enlist
Father Ryan's sympathy. Instead of sympathy, he gave me a
prescription, "If you feel nervous, and there's no reason why

you should in this friendly little group, say a prayer to the Holy Ghost, concentrate on your subject, and forget about yourself."

To pray was easy enough. To concentrate on my subject, when my stomach was roiling, was more difficult. I stood before the class, mute with fear.

"The prayer . . ." Father Ryan prompted, smiling up encouragingly from the front row.

I said a prayer.

"Now concentrate on your subject."

I tried to recall the photograph, the gaunt face, in the encyclopedia. To the face I matched whatever it was I had extracted from the biography, slightly more comprehensible than the *Britannica* article, that Father Ryan had lent me. The sole fact I retain about Newman from this episode is that he was the author of "Lead, Kindly Light." I think I made a good deal of this bit of information. A voice emanated from my throat. It was an octave lower than the one my ears were accustomed to. Still, it could be heard, and I didn't trip over my words or roll them into a ball. What my address lacked in urbanity, it made up for in brevity. It was very, very brief. My hungry clubmates, who were not allowed to open their lunch boxes until I'd finished, were so grateful that, at the end of the meeting when club officers were chosen, they elected me president.

"You see?" Father Ryan said triumphantly. "Timid, indeed! Why, you have the makings of a public speaker. You ought to consider running for class officer."

A public speaker? A class officer? The young curate gave me a new view of myself. Following my modest success at the Newman Club, I began to try to make up for my deficiencies in class assignments and on tests by shining in oral work. Because there were so many students of foreign-born parents at George Washington, considerable attention was given to public speaking. At the annex we read Burke's speech *On*

Conciliation, and were required to prepare an argument, modeled on Burke, to deliver before the class. It was such an important assignment that the mark received for it counted for half the final grade. The question was, what subject to select? The previous year Marie had pleaded the cause of Mary Queen of Scots. Her passionate arguments, rehearsed on me, had easily convinced me that Queen Elizabeth was a cold-hearted villain (it was years before I could take a larger view of her), who had unjustly accused Mary Stuart of treason. If I took the same subject, about which I'd picked up a good deal of information during the rehearsals, I would have a minimum of reading to do. I had an advantage over many of my classmates, who heard no English at home or heard it spoken ungrammatically, in that I could count on the agreement of subjects with predicates and forms of irregular verbs to come out correctly. When my turn came, I tried with all my might to think of Mary's debonair courage before the hangman at Fotheringham Castle, instead of the cowardice of the girl trembling before a gum-chewing, foot-shuffling, unruly class of adolescents.

After I passed with flying colors, which meant I would squeak through English with a "D," word got around that I was able to speak before groups. The following semester, backed by my pals on the basketball team and the Newman Club, I was elected president of the class. In those days of token self-government, my duties, which consisted of greeting my fellow students in the hall with a breezy "Hi!" and deciding whether we should send a contingent up the hill to the stadium to represent us at the next football game, didn't weigh heavily on me — except, once a month, when I had to lead the assembly. The student government's faculty advisor, instructing me in how to conduct my first appearance before the entire freshman class, said, "After the salute to the flag and the singing of the national anthem, you walk to the lectern, wait for complete silence — that's very important —

and then read the selection from the Bible I will have marked. After the reading, you introduce . . ."

I had ceased listening. Had I realized that reading aloud would be one of my jobs, I, of course, would not have run for office. Terrified at the prospect, I confessed that I couldn't read aloud.

"Rubbish," she said. "You don't have to be an actress. All I'm asking you to do is read."

"All I'm asking you to do is read." She made it sound so easy. I'd thought I wouldn't be able to speak before a group and I had been able to. Who knew? I might be able to read aloud after all. I hadn't tried it in so long, I was able to live through the days before the first assembly by telling myself that some magic would make it possible. When the time came, I walked to the front of the stage in a kind of trance, waited for silence and looked down at the Bible. A white light, like a flash bulb, went off in front of my eyes. I gripped the lectern to steady myself. As the light cleared I saw the marked passage rise and fall, twist and turn as if it were on a piece of paper floating under water.

Later, I heard that the advisor, who was sitting on the stage with the class officers, whispered to the vice-president to take over. He unclamped my hands from the lectern, led me to my chair, and read the Scripture.

Since no one understood the real cause of my paralysis, teachers and classmates alike went out of their way to comfort and reassure me.

"Poor thing . . ."

"Stage fright."

"Can happen to anyone."

"Even Lily Pons . . ."

The faculty advisor agreed from then on to give me the Bible selection two days in advance of each assembly. I worked over the passage (with help from Marie for words I didn't know), then memorized it. As in the days of play-acting at reading in first grade, I had to remember to keep my eyes down as I "read," only occasionally looking up at the audience, to maintain the illusion that I was giving an impromptu performance. Always afraid my memory might fail, and that I'd be thrown back on the printed words, I died a little at every assembly and continued to do so throughout my career as a politician.

At the beginning of sophomore year class officers were moved up the hill, together with students whose averages put them in the upper quarter of the class, a year before the rest of the sophomores. The Main Building was an agreeable contrast to the annex. Its site, on the highest point of land for miles around (a steep climb up from Academy Street, a pleasant walk down), gave its occupants a feeling of being surrounded by air and light. The building's colonial façade, its large playing field, and stadium made George Washington resemble a suburban high school more closely than a city institution. The dominant style of dress and manner among the students imitated, in the degree to which they could afford it, college campus life. There were football games and cheerleaders, there were Friday afternoon dances to which one wore black crew-necked sweaters, bobby socks, and saddle shoes, there were proms in a decorated gymnasium to which girls wore evening gowns and corsages of gardenias, and boys wore borrowed tuxedos. There were commencements at which hand-picked girls, dressed in Martha Washington costumes and carrying garlands, led the procession, while the band played Handel's "Largo."

Euphoric though the premature move up the hill made me, it had the disadvantage that it separated me from the underground at the same time that it threw me into classes with the intellectual élite. Since I had squeaked by the first year mostly by cribbing and copying, I was afraid that without the help of organized crime I would be lost. On the other hand, my delinquent behavior had begun to seem so reprehensible once I'd taken office that I was relieved to be forced to go straight.

Surprisingly, and for reasons that were obscure to me at the time, my grades began to improve. The previous summer I'd gone to Long Island for vacation fresh from my political triumphs — triumphs I interpreted as meaning: You're not a total flop — feeling better about myself than I had since I began public school. My increased self-confidence showed. Boys began to pay attention to me. One of them, likening my hair to the color of an Irish setter's coat, called me "Rusty." I seized it as a nickname. A new name would magically make me a new person. Eileen had a dreary past; Rusty a bright future. To complete the transformation, I changed the style of my handwriting. The Palmer Method slant to the right being associated with my unhappy days in elementary school, I trained my pen in what I thought was a fashionable and emancipated backhand. A touch of Tangee lipstick when Auntie wasn't looking, a few words borrowed from Marie's Westchester vocabulary, and the new me was ready for the new academic year.

At a period when many of my classmates were suffering the torments of adolescence, I began to flourish. My health was better than it had ever been. I was not moody and irritable like so many my age; how could I be when I felt I had escaped from jail? There was always, always, the vague uneasiness that I would be caught, but the farther we moved academically from subjects in which basic skills were taught, the less chance there was of that. Geometry, depending more on reasoning and less on arithmetic computation, was easier for me than algebra. Biology was an uncontaminated and interesting subject. In history I made up for poor reading comprehension of textbook assignments by being attentive in class. Intelligent questions took me a long way in civics.

English was my downfall. It kept me chained to the past.

On book reports the teacher wrote "Sp." after every third word, and next to the grade — usually 55 or 60 — asked, "Did you really understand what this book is *about?*" The answer to which was, of course, that I did not. Since I had not read the book, and had based the report on interviews with others who had read it, her question was a charitable way of saying: You're bluffing.

It was not in English class that I made progress toward literacy but in Latin. Because Latin consonants, vowels, and their combinations represent predictable sounds, and the spelling is not capricious and tricky, I had a friendly feeling toward Latin. I didn't tune out when the teacher taught us about prefixes and suffixes, about infinitives, gerundives, and subordinate clauses. I even began to enjoy playing with words and sprinkled my conversation, often inappropriately, with Latin phrases. If I said that a boy was "e pluribus unum," what I meant was that he was one in a million. "Make it snappy," I translated loosely into "Quam celer-rime." And that conversational crutch "No kidding!" became a more urbane "Mirabile dictu!" I rolled these newly learned sounds around on my tongue as if they were exotic jujubes. It was through this playing with words, I think, that I learned to blend sounds in reading. This blending, carried over from Latin to English, helped me finally to make "fetch" out of "fe etch." I don't say that I was good in Latin, for I wasn't; only that it was good for me. Through Latin, though I didn't realize it at the time, I took a giant step toward becoming a reader.

Except in English, where only my oral work pulled me through, my grades improved. This improvement, as I was uneasily aware, was only partly merited. The other part was the result of the "halo effect" — an impressionistic judgment of ability based on inference rather than performance. To make up for my daydreaming and laziness in preparing homework assignments, especially reading assignments which quickly put me to sleep, I was more attentive in class than many of my fellow students. My eager attentiveness together with my success in politics affected the way my teachers judged my work. In making up grades, when they could, and they often could, they gave me the benefit of the doubt. Should it be 65 or 70? Based on tests and homework grades, 65. Remembering how I kept my eyes fixed on them in class, drinking in what they said, they decided I deserved a 70. Maybe even 75. I looked bright, therefore I was. They wanted me to do well, among other reasons because if my average dropped too low, I would not be allowed to run for office again, and who knew what kind of troublemaker would be elected in my place?

With the one teacher who thought extracurricular activities a waste of time, Dr. Bice, a scholarly man with a goatee, who looked and behaved more like a college professor than a high school teacher of Latin, I wore the halo of being my sister's sister. His assumption that I would do well, his perplexed, almost wounded look when I did not, made me take care never to go to his class unprepared.

Ray Tara, a brain who sat next to me in Latin, created the pleasing myth that I was bright enough to do well, had my extracurricular activities (which had now reached fever pitch: captain of the fencing and basketball teams as well as president of the class) allowed me sufficient time for preparation. He suggested we do our homework together. That way I'd be sure of getting it done. "It's an ablative absolute, don't you think?" he'd say, as if my judgment were every bit as good as his.

"Unhuh," I'd agree, trying to concentrate on what Caesar was up to instead of tracing with my eyes the curve of Ray's upper lip. What a shame Ray didn't dance.

I tried to get Ray to dance. He tried to get me to read. *Ben Hur* was a book I wouldn't be able to put down, he said. I knew very well I wouldn't be able to pick it up. Although I had said breezily that I would sometime read another in the Outdoor Girl series, that time had yet to come. To read for pleasure never occurred to me — until Easter vacation my sophomore year.

I remember the occasion clearly, as one does when one performs an important and unaccustomed act. It was in the house of our Westchester relatives. Uncle Charlie was down in his Maiden Lane office, Aunt Hilda was out shopping, and Marie, my built-in companion, was upstairs in bed with a cold. Heavy rain kept me indoors. I wandered from room to room, ate a piece of fruit, picked out a tune on the piano, looked over the window, flopped down in a wicker chair on the sun porch. Rain! For one who lacked inner resources there was *nothing to do.*

On the glass-topped table next to the chair was a score pad for bridge. In my new backhand, I made a list of my current crushes. Ray Tara led the rest. I played a solitary game of tic-tac-toe. With little interest, I looked at the book the pad had been resting on. *Years of Grace* it was called. At one time there had been a lot of talk about it at the dinner table. A bestseller, it had been read by everyone in the house — except, of course, me. Afterward, it had been relegated to the bookcase on the sun porch. I was about to put it back where it belonged. But then, remembering that I had nothing else to do, I flipped through its pages. Chapters entitled "André" and "Jimmy" reminded me of an earlier vacation and of an unanswered question. During the Christmas holiday the year I was in eighth grade, Marie and I were invited to Jimmy Doyle's house for the afternoon. We had played with Jimmy's new chemistry set, making malodorous concoctions, and were having a boisterous game of round-robin Ping Pong when Mrs. Doyle called us to come to the dining room for a "little tea party." There was an awkward moment when it became clear that the French boy from up the street, who had been among those playing with us, was not being invited to the table. Since I had been quite taken with André's dark good looks and his silky accent, and much preferred him to chubby and unexotic Jimmy, I was saddened and puzzled by his exclusion. The expression on André's face as he turned away, pretending he didn't care, came between me and the splendid refreshments.

A plate of sugar hearts, colored red for the season, was passed around after the dainty sandwiches. At the end of the meal, I slipped one of the hearts out of the dish and was wrapping it in my handkerchief when I felt Mrs. Doyle's eyes on me. She gave me a long, questioning look and said, "That's all right, dear. You may have it. Why don't you eat it now?"

It was not for me, I blurted out.

"For whom is it then?"

Embarrassed by what I was afraid she would take as a criticism of her behavior, I fumbled and stuttered and tried to beg off answering. When it was clear that she wouldn't let me join the others until I confessed, I admitted it was for André.

"Well, then," she said coldly, taking the candy from my hand, "we'll just put it back on the table, shall we?"

What was wrong with André? Aunt Hilda was evasive. She said perhaps André was not the Doyles's "sort." Whatever did that mean? His elegant manners made Jimmy and the other boys who had been at the tea party seem like ruffians. I puzzled over this episode for some time and then forgot about it. The startling coincidence of finding those two names as chapter headings in *Years of Grace* aroused my curiosity again.

The "André" chapter, which opens the book, begins with dialogue. Good. I like dialogue. It goes quickly. Jane and André, on whom she has a crush, are in high school. So am I. Jane is fifteen. So am I. She daydreams about dances. So do I. André wears a beret. He is going to be an artist when he grows up. He'll live in Paris. He is so attractive (in an interesting way), and so gallant with Jane, that I am falling in love with him. The author leads me to believe that sooner or later he will kiss Jane — i.e., me. I hurry on, skipping descriptions, of which there are mercifully few, to the section where Jane and André go on an evening picnic. André's parents are with them. Now why did the author bring them along? Won't they be in the way? My impatience is growing. After a tedious interlude, during which André's father sings, "Au clair de la lune," Jane and André go for a walk. Alone. At last!

> "Jane — you *do* love me?" said André.
> Jane only wept the more.
> "Kiss me," said André.
> She raised her lips to his. The ground fell away from under her feet. The world was no more. Nothing existed but just — herself and — André.
> "My love," he said again.

The world was no more for me either. Torrid love scenes in movies had not affected me so strongly. They were about gangsters' molls, spies, and sirens. This is about *me*. There is no question of stopping now.

When teachers had tried to interest me in reading by saying, "One learns so much from books," I had thought they meant one learned so many facts, as in, "Your thinking is muddled. You've got to get the facts straight." Facts, except the facts of life, didn't interest me. What interested me was the way people behaved. And why. Why, for example, was Aunt Hilda's neighbor, Mrs. Bradbury, who had such an attractive and seemingly attentive husband, having an affair with another man? I had a feeling Margaret Ayer Barnes knew the answers, and would let me in on some of the secrets of life.

Spring rains and my sister's illness continued for most of the vacation. I read on and on. From time to time Aunt Hilda looked into the sun porch and put her hand to my forehead. Never having seen me read before, she suspected that I was coming down with the cold that had laid Marie low. The only reality for me now was between the covers of my book. The rest of life was a jarring interruption.

André promises Jane's mother, a narrow-minded woman who is dead against him because he's a foreigner and a Catholic, that he won't write to Jane until she's twenty-one. He goes off to Paris. Jane goes to college, makes her debut, meets a nice American Protestant, whom her mother is crazy about, and, two chapters later, marries him. This unromantic match, as unsuitable as Jo's to Mr. Bhaer in *Little Women*, vexed me so much that I threw the book down. The next day, remembering that there was a chapter called "Jimmy," I picked it up again. While the original André had long since vanished from my life, Jimmy Doyle, considerably slimmed down, was very much in it.

The Jimmy in the novel is a composer, married to a college friend of Jane's. When his concerto is played in Chicago, he visits Jane. They begin an affair. Aha! (I'd never heard the word "affair" used in this way until a few days earlier when Aunt Hilda was gossiping with a friend over tea and here it was again.) Jane's affair with Jimmy is rather confusing. What exactly is going on? Is it that the writing is becoming more difficult? Or is it that the strain, the fatigue of reading a whole book is beginning to tell? After ten pages or so I suddenly realize I haven't read a word. My mind has been a blank. Well, not really a blank, come to think of it. Haven't I been having a daydream about the real Jimmy? My daydream (which I am aware of perhaps for the first time) is much more interesting than what the author is saying at the moment. I'm not reading *and I know it*. I finish my daydream, skip the Jimmy section, and hurry to the end. Surely André will appear again and Jane will see what a mistake she made not to marry him.

André does indeed appear in the last chapter. When Jane goes to Paris with her husband, she meets André, who is now a famous sculptor. He invites her to his studio. As she looks over his statues — all nudes! — she realizes that each one is a *different* woman. How right her mother was! Jane realizes that André is not her sort; she could never have been happy with him.

No, no, no! I protested, feeling cheated. Did a reader have no recourse against an author? Before the end of the vacation I thought of a way to take revenge on Margaret Ayer Barnes, Jane's mother, and Mrs. Doyle. To cleanse the bad taste left in my mouth by the scene in the studio, I reread the opening chapter up to the ground-fell-away-from-Jane's-feet scene. When I closed the book, Jane and André were young again. And in love.

Slowly, very slowly, and without being aware of doing so, I had picked up the skills, and equally important, the self-confidence that made it possible for me to read. What I had been lacking was the motivation. The rain, the separation from my sister and other companions, the unanswered question about Mrs. Doyle's incomprehensible behavior, and a novel written in a straightforward, undemanding style, whose heroine I identified with, provided the necessary inducement.

Following this vacation, whenever my wildly extroverted life, which was filled with activities infinitely more appealing, allowed, I read. I didn't read easily, I didn't by any means understand everything I read, I didn't develop the habit of reading, but I read. *Years of Grace* had done for me what a solo cross-country automobile trip does for the beginning driver. Having driven through the novel to the end, with no prodding by anyone, carried along by interest and excitement, I was tired but exhilarated. I had overcome my fear of books. While I didn't "love" them, as my sister did, I no longer hated them. Like the beginning drivers, my skills, though barely up to the undertaking at the beginning, had improved considerably by the end. And like the driver, who even after a long trip is likely for some time to be cautious and selective about routes, my taste in books was narrow and finicky. Novels about ancient Rome, which fitted in well with my carefully disguised erotic fantasies (I was a *matrona Romana*, or a Christian for love of whom a pagan general and his entire army become converted), interested me more than those whose settings were the misty heaths and barren moors of the British Isles. Or was it that my prejudice against English was still so strong, and the books on the English list so connected in my mind with those dreaded book reports, that for pleasure I turned to the list of recommended reading for Latin class — to *Ben Hur, Boadicea,* and *The Last Days of Pompeii*?

In my junior and senior years, when I began to see my teachers as larger-than-life heroes and heroines, whose mannerisms, styles of dressing, and private lives were more interesting than those of movie stars, I rode on waves of inspirational teaching from class to class, and my grades rose still higher. As I had wanted to please Dr. Bice, I now wanted to please them all. The pronunciation of French was so important to Mademoiselle Faforgue that I stood before the mirror each evening gargling the *r* for half an hour as she'd urged us to do. I worked hard at Cicero to please Miss Walsh. Because I so much admired Miss Jamison, I struggled to understand *Twelfth Night,* muddle though it was. Economics, as taught by Mr. Gottesman, intrigued me because he promised that his subject would explain the advent and disappearance of the Apple Man who, from time to time, still haunted my dreams.

It was Mr. Gottesman who urged me to major in economics in college. A few in the class, like Ray Tara, won scholarships they could afford to take. I would be going to a city college. I had heard from my sister how little it resembled the rahrah colleges of raccoon coats and chrysanthemums one saw in the movies and that I remembered from my summer in Hanover. So the final semester of comparative freedom was precious to me. In the office where the student government, of which I was now president, held court with the class officers, star athletes, and chief brains, we loitered late, to prolong each day. When the janitor came to lock up for the night and shooed us out, we walked down the hill, arms linked, six or eight abreast in the road, singing George Washington songs at the top of our lungs in a delirium of school spirit, feeling we might burst with the sweetness of life.

Only when I was alone, and I was alone very little, did my uneasiness about "passing" intrude on my happiness or cast a shadow over my future. Because others seemed to be unaware of the limits of my literacy, I tended to forget them. Still, there were always disquieting reminders. In the last hectic week before commencement, I had to remember to get from the student government advisor the selection from the Scriptures and memorize it.

After the playing of Handel's "Largo," I "read" (eyes on the lectern, but looking up at the audience from time to time) what was, and has remained for me, an especially moving passage from the Book of Wisdom:

Wherefore I prayed, and understanding was given me:
I called upon God, and the spirit of wisdom came to me.
I preferred her before sceptres and thrones
And esteemed riches nothing in comparison with her.
Neither compared I unto her any precious stone,
Because all gold in respect of her is as a little sand,

And silver shall be counted as clay before her.
I love her above health and beauty,
And chose to have her instead of light:
For the light that cometh from her never goeth out.

Chapter VIII

. . . desperate, doomed people . . . bewildered by their failure (they had been assigned to this course because they were far below average in English), unable to comprehend his teaching, his encouragement, his love. Their failure had widened their eyes, given them the alert, electric look of animals to whom all movements signal danger. Like animals, they appeared mild and obedient until, knowing themselves trapped, they slashed out at him as if he were the crystalization of the forces that had maimed them — the obscure, mysterious spirit of the famous university itself, so available to them (they with their high-school diplomas), and yet as it turned out, so forbidden to them, its great machinery ever now working, perhaps, to process cards, grades, symbols that would send them back to their families and the lives they supposed they had escaped.

"Archways," by Joyce Carol Oates, in
Upon the Swooping Flood and Other Stories

Life for the 1200 freshmen, all women, entering Hunter College with me, was sweet only in the lyrics of popular songs. The majority of them, daughters of working-class parents, looked upon the free education the city offered those who qualified as a step to be taken as quickly as possible, without soft lights or music, to enable them to earn a living and contribute to the support of their families. What time was left them after classes they devoted not to football games and proms but to part-time jobs and peace marches. And had any of them had leisure, they would not have been tempted to loiter in the provisional quarters — tenements, office buildings, and lofts — in which classes were held. Whatever the decision made by the legislators about allocating funds for a new building, the members of my class knew that, except for the year we would spend on a treeless site in the northern reaches of the Bronx, our campus would be the college cafeteria and the city sidewalks.

In a decrepit converted factory, leaning in the shadow of the Third Avenue El, we were squeezed so tightly, it was risky to make an expansive gesture. We pushed and shoved our way through the door and up the stairwells (the elevator was permanently out-of-order). We pushed and shoved our coats and overshoes into narrow lockers. We pushed and shoved our way into the library and lunchroom where, with luck, we might share a seat with only one other person. Our classrooms were airless and overheated in winter. In spring and fall, when the windows were open, they reeked of the coffee being roasted in neighboring factories.

At the Lexington Avenue Synagogue, which had been lent

the college for assemblies, my friends and I from George Washington were overwhelmed at the size of the class when we saw it en masse. The opening remarks of the dean of freshmen were intimidating. She warned us that we were in for a painful "period of adjustment," and that those whose grades fell below the required level would be dropped at the end of the first semester. When she turned the meeting over to the student government, we listened, awe-struck, as one candidate for office after another presented a platform on which she hoped to be elected. These girls — women rather — whose parents had been educated politically by the trade unions to which they belonged had, in their high schools, been debating not about Mary Stuart and Queen Elizabeth but about Trotsky and Stalin. Their vocabularies crackled with words like "agitation," "petition," "protest," "fink," and "scab."

By the time my name was called in nomination (by a friend sitting in the balcony and therefore out of reach), the confidence I had built up as a public speaker at George Washington had evaporated. Only reluctantly did I mount the dais, aware, by now, that the governing of this student body would require more than breezy greetings and bright smiles. The last of ten nominees to speak, I had considerable time to fret about not having a platform. Like everyone else I was for world peace. And of course I saw the need for a new college building. What about the other "issues"? When, after the long and passionate addresses made by the others, my turn came, I admitted candidly that I had no position on the other issues; I would have to study them to find out where I stood.

The election of a dark horse from what was considered a country club high school took everyone by surprise — not least of all the skittish dark horse. (An analysis of the balloting, conducted by the two major parties representing powerful groups from the serious high school, purportedly showed that disaffection with familiar leaders had made would-be supporters cast their votes for a stranger: Time for a change, they had decided. My private theory was that it was the brevity of my speech that, as in the election at the Newman Club, had brought me victory.) When I breathlessly reported my triumph at home, Auntie, who had never disguised her lack of enthusiasm for my extracurricular successes, which she saw as time-wasters and possible head-turners, looked up from the book she was reading just long enough to say, "Do you realize your skirt is on crooked?"

A week later when I announced that my class had collected money to send me to Washington as a delegate to a peace demonstration, she put her book down. Whistling her "Tssss," she considered whether to let me go, wondering if she shouldn't have listened to Grandmother and sent us to a "nice" (i.e., private) college. Marie, who had been growing increasingly rebellious at home, had recently refused, under the influence of her political science teacher, to cross the picket line at the Dyckman Street bakery. And now her younger sister, who had never had a thought in her head, was asking to go to the nation's capital on a Communist-inspired demonstration. Instead of refusing permission outright, Auntie expressed her disapproval with the increasingly familiar phrase, "Use your own judgment." I struggled under this chilly and burdensome formula overnight. The following day I was seen off by my rowdy friends who had not yet taken it in that the giddy high school days were over.

Beginning with the all-night coach ride, the days of rallies, calls on senators, congressmen, lobbyists, and union leaders, there was hardly a moment in the next six months when someone was not indoctrinating me "on the issues." Nor did I have a respite in class, for my major and minor, economics and political science, were extremely popular with the politically sophisticated students. Our professors were often thrown into the role of referee as Trotskyites, members of the

Young Communist League, and Socialists battled for domination. The discussions were so heated they often continued after the bell had rung to announce the end of the period, when, still shouting and gesticulating at one another, we pushed and shoved our way down the stairwell and out into the street.

If these classes were too high-pitched to be agreeable, they nevertheless gave me the feeling that bubbles were bursting in areas of my brain I hadn't known existed. And after the month or so it took me to learn the new vocabulary and tactics, I was as vocal and combative as the others. Keyed up and hoarse, I'd go to English class and feel intellectual excitement funnel into panic. Freshman English was written English: no possibility of talking my way into a passing grade in this one. Each week we were required to write a theme on an assigned subject. These essays were far more difficult for me than the dreaded book reports had been in high school because there was no way I could fill up my paper with phrases, sentences, and even paragraphs "borrowed" (i.e., copied wholesale) from the books. I was on my own. My written vocabulary, limited as it was to words I thought I had a chance of spelling correctly, allowed me to express my ideas in only the most simplified way. What I put down on paper, with anxious impatience, seemed to me so childish that after a paragraph or two I ran dry. All week I'd sit over my introduction, paralyzed by what I took to be a lack of imagination. Thursday evening in desperation I'd put something down to fill up the required number of pages — this something full of misspellings for all my sidestepping around "difficult" words — and, cringing at the way it exposed my illiteracy, hand it in.

Math 101, a combination of analytical geometry, calculus, and trigonometry, followed English. (On my own I certainly wouldn't have taken mathematics. Like Latin and German it was one of the requirements in an inflexible course of study which offered little freedom of choice, apart from a major and minor, until junior year.) A glance at the textbook filled me with dread: logarithms and mile-long equations. I listened hard to the professor's explanation of how to solve a problem, but, after working on an equation for some time, I'd realize that I must have miscopied part of it from the blackboard. Or, farther along in my calculations, I had left out, or doubled, a row of figures. I'd frantically cross out my work and begin again. In the meantime the class had moved on to the next problem and the next. On my way home on the subway, in the evening, in my dreams at night, I covered reams of paper with calculations that led nowhere.

Even in my major and minor subjects, which I was supposedly "good at," things were going badly. Note-taking, which I had not had to do in any serious way before, made my brain ache. Dividing my attention between listening and writing was as demanding as hitting my head with one hand while making circles on my stomach with the other. If the professor's delivery was rapid, and the material dense, which was usually the case, I found that when my notes were cold they made as little sense as spirit-writing. What had I meant to put down here? The spelling was so fantastical that I couldn't guess what I had intended. Surely the digits in this crucial statistic about the war debt were scrambled. And instead of the name of the Secretary of the Treasury, what I'd written was the name of my neighbor who'd asked to borrow a pencil. To compound my chagrin I couldn't count on my memory for what had been said because I'd been so busy writing I hadn't been able to concentrate on listening.

My initial feverish attempt to keep up with my classes was followed by a period when I pretended to myself that I was keeping up. Disorganization, a feeling of being messy and dirty (my papers *were* messy and dirty from so many erasures, crossings-out, and writings-over) made it an easy slide into lethargy, with a massive loss of confidence. Where had I got the inflated notion that there were subjects I was "good at" when I didn't seem capable of a task as mechanical as note-taking? No brain work required there: just writing down what one heard — which any clerk could do. What was I doing in college? Especially this college, where, as I was discovering, one was penalized in all courses for spelling errors on examinations.

How, I began to wonder, had I got through high school? The false sense of academic security I'd been lulled into at George Washington was shattered in a highly competitive milieu where students were a last name, where no one wore a halo, where there were no favorites, and where grades, as one was constantly reminded, were all important. There were grades on recitations, grades on quizzes, grades on examinations, grades on term papers. Grades were converted into an index. Whether a student would be permitted to continue with her major depended upon her index. Whether she would be permitted to hold office depended on her index. Whether she would be permitted to stay in college depended on her index.

What was I doing here if grades were all important? For weeks on end I was so befogged with feelings of worthlessness and self-doubt that I was deaf to what was going on in class. My gloomy ruminations consumed me. It took a particularly raucous debate in economics to shake me out of my self-absorption. Out of the corner of my ear I heard an assertion that seemed to me so wrong-headed — was it that religion was the opiate of the masses? — that I was drawn into the battle.

The excess of adrenalin left over after the discussion was broken up by the arrival of the next class permitted me to take stock of my situation. In some subjects my brain *did* work. In others it did not. In English I was certain to fail. Dr. Williams, returning my latest theme, had said, "This won't do, you know." I knew, and knew also that she meant not just this theme, but all the work I'd handed in so far. As there was no way I could write on a level that would be acceptable to her, I decided to give up the weekly agony. I continued to go to class, but I was doing time. In Math 101 I continued to make a feeble attempt. Latin and German I would squeak by in. It was in my major and minor that I still had a chance of doing well. Since note-taking eroded what self-confidence I had, I decided to abandon it. Listening attentively had got me by before; why not now? With a student who was in both these classes I made a bargain: If she would lend me her notes once a week so that I could copy out the important facts and figures, I would teach her to dance. (She was as astonished to find a college freshman who couldn't take notes as I was to find an eighteen-year-old girl who couldn't dance.)

The term papers in these subjects while difficult for me were not impossible. Whenever I could I chose a subject that required field work — visits to the municipal courts for political science, a morning at the New York Stock Exchange for economics. Reportage, a flat-footed account of my observations, was within my ability (whereas the "imaginative" writing needed for themes was not). Field work also provided a sanctioned alternative to the library. One could see the courts at work or one could read about how they worked. For me the choice was clear. One was full of human interest, the other dry as the paper it was written on. I enjoyed interviewing lawyers, judges, listening in on trials. I could rarely get by without doing some reading for a paper, but after the field work, I was able to visualize what I read in the text and, incidentally, borrow the necessary vocabulary and correct spelling. (It was a "bear" not a "bare" market.)

When the indexes were computed at the end of the first semester, the size of the class was reduced by a third. Among those told not to return were all but two of my high school friends. Thanks to B's in my major and minor, I was allowed to remain — with three provisos. These the dean of freshmen rapped out to me: I must give up the presidency of the class and all other extracurricular activities; I must repeat mathematics which I had failed; I must take a noncredit course, called by the students "Idiot English," designed for refugees from Europe who needed additional help with English.

How much my poor showing had disappointed the faculty, the dean told me more than once. Although my entrance examination had been far from brilliant, recommendations from my high school teachers had led the admissions office to expect great things of me: I would be a "leader." Through a want of application, I was allowing the presidency to fall into the hands of an "agitator," and had narrowly escaped the ignominy of being dropped. It had been decided that I should be given one more chance on the theory that if I could do well in some subjects, I should be able to do well in all of them. However, if I didn't put my nose to the grindstone, there was every likelihood that at the end of the next semester (when there would be another mass expulsion) I would join the others who were now out on the streets looking for jobs.

There was nothing I wanted more than to leave college and begin working. As I watched my friends empty their lockers, I felt like an inmate in a reform school watching others be discharged. Had it not been for the dread I would have felt at presenting Auntie with the news that I had been dropped, I would have rejoiced at being able to give up the struggle. In a way my failure was a relief. From fourth grade on I'd been bracing for it. Here it was at last. No more social promotions, no more getting by on being a goody-goody, a clown, or a politician. I had been judged on my ability and had failed. Why not listen to the warning and clear out?

If I accepted the provisos and remained in college, what was there to look forward to? I would probably be able to pass mathematics in summer school where, it was rumored, grading was somewhat more lenient. That left "Idiot English." Suppose, by some fluke, I passed that, and got by another semester, what I had to look forward to was years of being imprisoned in overcrowded classrooms and airless libraries. Years of so-called vacations during which one labored over term papers. Years of grinding worry about the next index, and the next. And to what purpose? To prepare for a career in teaching I was almost certain I didn't want.

"Type or teach — which will it be?" Auntie had asked when time came to decide for or against the pedagogy courses Hunter offered as an adjunct to the liberal arts curriculum. When my eyes failed to light up at either possibility, she had said, "You didn't think you could dance your way through life, did you?"

I didn't say so, but I had rather hoped I could. During my high school days when I should have been bent over book reports, I was practicing Ginger Rogers pivots and twirls in front of a full-length mirror. In my junior and senior years, when I was allowed to go to dances with Marie on Friday nights, we Cariocaed across the gymnasium floor (as often as not with me forced into the Astaire rather than Rogers role because the boys stood around, gawking, leaving the girls to partner each other). Or we did the Peabody, Lindy, Big Apple, the Tango, whatever was in fashion, as soon as it was in fashion, at the parish house of a church in Inwood to which came serious dancers from all over the city.

If my appetite for dancing was undiminished by the time Auntie and I had the discussion, a time when I was going to the Glen Island Casino with my Westchester cousins and to the Savoy Ballroom in Harlem on dates, the twinges I'd begun to feel in my lower back had made me suspect that I was suffering from more than growing pains, and that I did not have the stainless steel spine necessary to be a professional dancer.

Being a secretary might not be bad, I thought, envisaging Joan Crawford or Claudette Colbert taking dictation in the boss's penthouse apartment. That was movie stuff, of course, and in our family one did not type; one taught. A dreary way to earn a living it seemed to me. With Auntie's social life revolving mostly around her colleagues, I had learned enough about the narrowness of the public school teachers' lives (in those days when few of them married and still fewer were men) to know the heavy price they paid for the famous security and long vacations. Besides, to teach economics in high school, the least repugnant of the possibilities open to one who had a horror of elementary schools, would mean remaining at home for the years it would take to qualify for the license exam, with no possibility of earning money. And, therefore, no independence.

Was this what I wanted, I asked myself as I commuted from Long Island to summer school repeating Math 101? Wouldn't it be better to get a job, any job? The question was academic, Auntie reminded me. Until I was of age, she, and not I, made the decisions. And it was her decision that, despite my poor showing, I must continue in college.

As summer was drawing to a close and the dreaded fall approached, I returned from the city one afternoon to find Auntie with news that couldn't wait until I put my books down: Marie had eloped. The separation Auntie had warned me would one day come had arrived and I was not much better prepared for it than I had been the year Marie had gone to Westchester to recuperate. The remainder of the summer is a blank. Did I go to the beach? Swim? Dance? Do all the summery things I had always done with Marie? Did I continue to delight in the warmth of the sun on my skin and the taste of salt air on my lips? I don't know. I remember only that without the companionship and support of my best friend and confidante (who had been on the Bronx campus, but was nevertheless at the same college), I more than ever dreaded the return to Hunter.

The year I was eighteen and a sophomore, through a series of losses, a radical change took place in my life, which, in turn, produced an equally radical, though less obvious, change in my personality. At home there was the loss of Marie. At college, the loss of extracurricular activities. And before long, there was the loss of the physical well-being I had enjoyed since high school. From having been physically active, emotionally dependent, and psychologically extroverted, I was forced almost overnight to become inactive, independent, and introverted. It was as if the rainy Easter vacation during which I had read *Years of Grace* had been extended from a week to a year. My built-in companion was not available, there was "nothing to do," and it might as well have been raining.

Auntie began to take seriously the back pain I had complained of off and on for two years the day she heard me refuse an invitation to a dance: Something must be gravely wrong. An orthopedist said the X rays showed I had a curvature of the spine. The pain was caused by pressure on the sciatic nerve for which he prescribed an extensive course of physiotherapy. The therapist he recommended had his offices in far-off Brooklyn. Three times a week I was to take the subway there and back, an hour and a half each way. When I complained that this would allow me little time to see my friends, Auntie said that was all to the good. The subway ride would give me nine hours of uninterrupted study time — if I used it properly.

And so it should have done. Characteristically I began each ride with good intentions, working, say, on a translation of the assigned passage from *Immensee* for my German class. Before the train had gone five stops, Storm's Teutonic romance and the motion of the car had lulled me into a torpor. Letting the novel fall on my lap, I slipped off into romances in which I was the heroine. I might have continued to squander the travel time in this way had I not come to see that my favorite daydreams had turned sour. What was the point of wishing the tall, bespectacled, studious-looking young man at the public library would ask to walk me home at closing time when the pain in my leg would begin to nag before we had gone three blocks? Even more frustrating would it be if he asked me to a prom. So constricted was my imagination that it did not occur to me to invent new fantasies in which physical activity, upon which heretofore so much of my pleasure had depended, was not important. Brooklyn began to seem as far away as Africa. How much longer would I have to continue treatment, I asked the therapist? There were no shortcuts in a case like mine, he said, irritable with me because I was not making progress. It might take six months, nine months. Maybe even a year.

A year! How would I be able to stand it? The boredom was almost worse than the pain. Boredom threw me back on the contents of my briefcase. Aside from texts, it contained books from the reading list for Idiot English, out-of-date, nonfiction best-sellers, selected because they were thought to be closer to the reading level of the students than *The Canterbury Tales* or *The Faerie Queene*.

Although I recognized that I wasn't literate enough to continue in the regular English course, I resented having to take Idiot English. This humiliation, which I took harder than my failure in math or my loss of the presidency, I concealed from my friends. I went to the room where the class met by an elaborately devious route, praying not to meet anyone I knew on the way, and blushed furiously if in casual conversation anyone mentioned the course's nickname. My resentment increased when, after the first week, I saw that the teaching would not be remedial in any way that would benefit me. I would not be taught techniques to improve my spelling, nor to find the words I wanted to express my thoughts. If it would give Europeans further drill in English grammar, it would do little for one whose disability was not easily pinpointed. Seeing the course as punitive rather than corrective, I sulked. I doodled and daydreamed instead of listening to the instructor, I never volunteered an answer to her questions, and I slipped back into my shifty high school habits of scanning a book to smoke out its subject, writing reports on which I got D's. An occasional F, with an acid reminder that failure to earn a satisfactory grade would mean I'd be dropped from college, would throw me into panic, for I both wanted and didn't want to be kicked out.

If it was panic that drove me to participate in class instead of sulking, it was the tediousness of the subway ride to Brooklyn that drove me deeper into Axel Munthe's *The Story of San Michele* than I would ordinarily have gone. Once I was into it, what Munthe had to say about doctors and patients (my current life) pulled me to the end. The next assignment, Noel Coward's *Present Indicative*, was so entertaining I thought it must have been put on the list by mistake. It was Romola Nijinska's biography of her husband that was the cause of my being late for an appointment: I had overshot the therapist's stop.

Six months of electrical treatments had a pernicious effect on my physical condition. The improvement in my reading, however, was considerable. By the time I had a scene with Auntie, in which I refused to continue with the therapist and asked to see another doctor, reading had become so agreeable a pastime that I continued doing the assignments after I stopped going to Brooklyn.

Without my being aware that it was happening, the books on the Idiot list established the habit of reading. When there was nothing to do — and without Marie, without sports, without politics, there often was nothing to do — I read.

These books also cured my allergy to libraries. I had begun going to the reading room of the Fordham branch of the public library with my friends to flirt with students from the men's colleges who worked there. After I stopped riding the subways to Brooklyn, I went every evening because I found that the quiet, the lack of motion, the bright lights, and silent companionship of others made a library an ideal environment for my new entertainment.

At the end of the semester, my English professor, still grumbling about the inexplicable discrepancy between my spoken and written English, wrote a favorable report on my progress. My index rose above, just above, the danger line. And the gelatinous mass between my third and fourth dorsal vertebrae reconstituted itself when nature was permitted to do her work without interference. The new orthopedist warned that I must not hurl myself into sports, so that summer, the first I was to spend in the city, looked as if it would be long and dull. I registered with the college employment office and waited to be called for a job.

Looking for a way to pass the time while I waited, I went to the neighborhood public library. It was a pleasant place with maple chairs and tables, large windows, and overhead fans. I looked over the shelves, wondering what to read. Without a list I was lost. I had no idea how to find what might interest me. Since the days of *Ben Hur* and *Boadicea* I had avoided fiction. What kept me from reading it now was that I had been told dogmatically by the English teacher to whom I had triumphantly reported having read *Years of Grace* that one did not have the right to read adult novels until one had completed the list of elementary and high school classics: *Treasure Island, Lorna Doone, Ivanhoe, Huckleberry Finn.* Sitting at the maple table, I made a valiant attempt to read them, but it was too late. I was too old for a first reading, too young for a second. There was an approachable-looking librarian. What about asking her for suggestions? Better not. The depth of my ignorance might shock her. I wandered over to the magazine rack. The *New Yorker* cartoons were funny, but the stories . . . Just as one was getting into them, they were over. And what, as Miss Shapiro, my sixth grade teacher would have asked, were they *about?* I studied the sinuous postures of the models in *Vogue* and read about high life in Manhattan — an agreeable pastime that quickly wore itself out.

When I complained at home that I was at loose ends, Auntie talked about inner resources, and lengthened the list of my chores. One of the new ones was to go every day or two to the drugstore lending library to select what Auntie called "reading matter" to feed her voracious appetite. In the beginning I found this job more onerous than shopping or doing the dishes. How could I choose a book for Auntie when I was incapable of choosing one for myself? I read the dust jackets, trying to decide what she would like, with little to go on, for although she was extremely articulate in general, when it came to judging books she favored one-word reviews. *Anthony Adverse* was "rubbish." *The Years* was "queer." *Of Time and the River* was "bloated." *Kitty Foyle* was "fluff." *Of Mice and Men* was "grim." Only once did my selection warrant an extended appraisal. "Whatever made you pick *this?*" she said, handing me back the book contemptuously. "Why, the man is . . . illiterate. He makes up words and misspells the way you do. Don't bring me anything else by this James Joyce. Let him go back to school and learn a thing or two before he takes up any more of my time."

A writer who made up words and didn't spell any better than I did. How interesting! On the way back to the drugstore a liberating thought occurred to me. I hadn't read the school classics: So what? Who was to keep me, now, from reading whatever I chose? Sitting on a stool at the soda fountain, and biting into a chocolate ice cream cone, I opened to a typography that told me this would be no ordinary novel: so much the better! The initial letter of the first word, a gigantic S, filled the left hand page. Nestled under it were the words "tately, plump."

> Stately, plump Buck Mulligan came down the stairhead, bearing a bowl of lather.

On the fourth word I tripped over my surname: Here was kinship indeed!
A few lines later,

> Introibo ad altare Dei

Familiar words. Then,

> Come up, Kinch. Come up, you fearful jesuit.

Also familiar. I could hear the line in the brogue Auntie mimicked so skillfully in stories about the old days in Chelsea. I read until the ice cream cone was finished, turned the book in, and went about my errands thinking of Buck and Stephen.

The next time I went to the drugstore, and from then on, I quickly chose a novel for Auntie, took what I was coming to think of as my book from the shelf, and sitting on a black metal chair behind a mountain of unopened cartons of Kleenex, continued reading.

Needless to say Joyce made greater demands on me than had Munthe or Noel Coward. There were whole chunks of *Ulysses* I could make nothing of. But neither could a great many other people. And unlike them, I had a high tolerance for incomprehension. I was not put off by the invented words (did I not invent words myself?) or bizarre spelling. I'd work at a page as I had worked at a translation from *Immensee* or *The Aeneid*. When I became discouraged, as I frequently did,

I had those shifty habits at the ready to help me cope: I skipped and flipped. The complex structure didn't trouble me because I didn't know it was there. I tried only to follow the story of Stephen, Bloom, and Molly. In many ways *Ulysses* was no harder for me than *Little Women* had been. And it was *much* funnier.

"Hey, what's so funny?" Mr. Kline, the druggist, would call from behind the apothecary jars. "Read me some."

I still couldn't read aloud. When I was forced to do it, I managed well enough if my auditor didn't have a copy of the text to follow and I was free to paraphrase. Or if the selection was simple, a newspaper story, for example. Joyce hardly fitted into this category. "It's in a brogue, I can't do a brogue," I lied.

At the beginning of August the college employment bureau sent me a card. I was to apply at Deb Dresses on Seventh Avenue for a modeling job. The owner, a nervous little woman named Mitzi, who kept her hat on indoors, said I was the right height and weight. Could she see my walk? My walk? Oh yes. I threw myself into the pelvic-thrust-forward, knees-pliés position I'd seen in *Vogue,* masked my face with what I hoped was a disdainful expression, and, carefully putting one foot in front of the other, made my way down the strip of carpet in front of the buyers' chairs. After a turn or two Mitzi asked me where I learned to walk like *that.* Still, at the moment she could not afford a professional model (the one who had been fired had departed in haste, leaving behind intriguing artifacts — falsies, an eyelash curler, a rainbow of lipsticks, pancake makeup — in the dressing room). Mitzi supposed that if I was smart enough to get into Hunter I should be smart enough to learn how to walk.

Deb Dresses was an undemanding job. In between fittings and the all-too-rare arrival of buyers and showings of the line of "jewel-toned" velveteen cocktail dresses, I ran to the

dressmakers' supply house for the seamstress and to the cafeteria for coffee for Mitzi. When I had nothing to do, I hid in
the closet that served as a dressing room, trying to pretend I
wasn't there, so Mitzi wouldn't remember that the most recent addition to the payroll was idle. On days when she and
the seamstress went out into the market, I sat at the desk to
answer a phone that rarely rang, and read the book I could
now afford to charge out of Mr. Kline's lending library.

Looking back, I see that I treated *Ulysses* on this first reading as a combination sex manual, script for a vaudeville act,
and song sheet:

> All dimpled cheeks and curls
> Your head it simply swirls
> Those girls, those girls
> Those lovely seaside girls

I'd sing on the way to buy straight pins and bias binding.

If Mitzi came back from the market and caught me with
Joyce, she'd say, "The bookworm's at it again. You're going
to get a squint. Who do you think will hire you when you
lose your looks?"

Her reproaches were music to my ears. A bookworm! No
one had ever called me that before.

Remembering that while she had been out I'd done nothing to earn my wages, she'd say, "Let me see you walk." To
give herself the illusion that there were customers, she and
the seamstress would sit in the showroom while I modeled
the velveteen dresses. "Shoulders back. Head up. Slow down
on the turns," Mitzi commanded between puffs on her cigarette.

If I hadn't already begun Molly Bloom's informative (when
it wasn't baffling) soliloquy, I was approaching it the day
Mitzi returned from a visit to her banker looking more nervous than ever. From her purse she took a tight little roll of
bills and peeled off some singles, the salary she owed me. She

was going into bankruptcy, she said stoically. She was afraid she'd have to let me go.

Sorry as I was to lose my first job, I had wondered how a house with so little business could afford to pay even slave wages to a model who sat at a desk and read. Thereafter, when my economics professors talked about marginal producers, I visualized Mitzi, a cigarette between her teeth, her hat firmly on her head, and hoped she had found a less nerve-wracking way to earn a living. I was grateful to her. She had given me my first job and a new view of myself. In Mitzi's eyes, and in Mitzi's eyes only, I was a brain.

The taste of money made me consider quitting college and getting a real job again. This time, I argued with myself that it would now be foolish to do so. Academically the worst was over. I had completed all the requirements that depended heavily on basic skills, and had survived what was known to be the most difficult years. I still depended heavily on listening (which a student can go a good deal further on than is generally imagined), but reading assignments and term papers had, through practice, become easier. So too had note-taking: One *can* learn to pat the head with one hand and make circles on the stomach with the other.

In my junior year, when for courses in logic, philosophy, and economic theory an ability to deal with abstractions was more important than knowledge based on previous education, my index rose sharply, and I enjoyed my classes. I even imagined that I was learning in the way good students learned because I earned good grades. It was only after I was out of college a year or two that I realized what a high price I had paid for depending so heavily on short-term memory and learning by ear. Memory traces that had not been reinforced by reviewing (which the good students did routinely but I never did), by reading as well as listening, faded so quickly that in a short time I had forgotten most of what I'd been taught as a freshman and sophomore (as, by

the time I'd reached college, I had forgotten a large proportion of what I had been taught in elementary and high
school). Getting by in college is one thing; learning another.

In an attempt to fill the void left after Marie married, I developed a band of close friends. Whereas formerly I had
sought only popularity (what need had I for closeness with
others when I had the perfect companion at home?), now
that Marie was living on Long Island, and seemed even farther away because she was an adult with a husband and
child while I was still a student, I fed my hunger for intimacy with what Auntie called "a cult of friendship."

In marathon talks in the cafeteria, my friends and I con-
fided in and advised one another on how to deal with the opposite sex, as well as how to perform in domestic psychodra-
mas. When two of the group took a popular course in the
novel, I found myself listening in on their literary discussions.
I listened as a penniless child looks into a candy store window. I would not have dared register for a course in the English Department.

("With *your* record?")

Was that any reason why I should not read the books?
Yvonne lent me her reading list. How seductive the titles
were to the eye! *Sons and Lovers, A Portrait of the Artist as a
Young Man, The Magic Mountain.* Since only those registered
for the course had the right to withdraw books on the reserve
shelf, Yvonne lent me the D. H. Lawrence novel, telling me
to read it quickly so that she could have it back by the due
date.

My enthusiasm suffered a check at the opening page. The
description of "The Bottoms" was drearily reminiscent of
my old bugbear, Thomas Hardy. Still, if the title was to be
trusted and the book was about lovers as well as sons . . . I
pushed on and was becoming increasingly caught up in Paul
Morel's life when, slow reader that I was, the book fell due. I

made what at the time seemed to me an extraordinary decision: I would buy the book. Leaving Altman's, where I had
taken a Saturday job as a salesgirl to pay for my clothes, I
stopped at a bookshop on 34th Street, my pay envelope in
hand, and asked for the Modern Library edition. As I paid for
it, and wrote my name and the date on the inside cover, I felt
I was making a commitment. What kind and where it would
lead I could not have said.

Finding my place, I continued where I'd left off. In some
mysterious way, owning the book increased my excitement
in what I read. Heart pounding, pulse racing, I stopped from
time to time to marvel at my unaccustomed speed and flu-
ency. I thought of a movie in which James Cagney, dancing
in the street, says euphorically, "Look at me. I'm dancin'!
I'm dancin'!" and shouted to myself, "Look at me. I'm reading! I'm reading!"

The Magic Mountain had for me, who had had a brush
with tuberculosis, a subject so compelling I felt I was spending my days at the International Sanatorium Berghof instead of at Hunter. I fought my way through the doldrums of
the philosophical debates, skipping when I was afraid of getting bogged down (and for the first time feeling ashamed of
doing so), pushing on eagerly, often cutting classes because I
couldn't bear to miss the discussion in the cafeteria. The rar-
efied air at Davos-Dorf affected all of us so much we greeted
one another each morning with a rundown of our symptoms —

"My temperature is elevated today."

"I have a hacky cough I can't get rid of."

"I didn't sleep last night."

"I'm *sure* I have t.b."

— like the inmates of the Berghof. And who of us did not
long to own a lacquered cigarette box, "with a troika going
full speed on the lid," and to drive men wild with languid
looks and insolent door-banging like Clavdia Chauchat?

Had any novel been able to augment my literary fervor, it would have been *A Portrait of the Artist*. No skipping here. This time, for the first time, I read every word. It was Joyce who stimulated my interest in Ireland. It was an easy jump from *Ulysses* and *A Portrait* to the Irish rebellion. Was I studying in the library at night or wandering in a Celtic twilight, filling my head with romantic foolishness? Auntie asked, when I questioned her about our ancestors. The latter. When I should have been outlining the works of Marx and Engels, I was reading the plays of Yeats and Lady Gregory.

In my senior year, I discovered in the catalogue a course on the novel-in-translation given in the German Department. It was typical of my continuing suspicion of everything connected with the for-so-long-hated subject of English that I approached reading in a crabwise fashion. Better to read the books on the Latin list in high school. Better now to read the books on a German Department list. Also, I suspected that the professor who taught the course, a European who'd recently joined the faculty, would neither know nor care that I had had to take Idiot English. No danger of being patronized.

("Are you *sure* you're up to the level of this course?")

When I went with my permission sheet to the German office, I found Dr. Arpad Steiner, a short, squat man with an enormous head that bobbed and swayed, tortoise-like, at the end of a long neck, sitting behind a mountain of leather-bound books. He'd be glad to have me in the class, he said, signing the form, but I must be warned that the novels he had selected were all long. With a schedule as demanding as mine, I would have to burn the midnight oil to keep up with the assignments.

My life that year was intimately associated with the Third Avenue El. From Theodore Roosevelt High School where I did a morning's stint of practice teaching (Fordham Road station), to college for afternoon classes (34th Street station), back up to Harlem where I worked evenings at a clinic (125th Street station), the El served me as a means of transportation, as restaurant, and as reading room. Boarding at Fordham Road at noon, I could look forward to an undisturbed hour, the only respite in an otherwise hectic day, of reading for Dr. Steiner's course. As the train snaked along like a sluggish, overstuffed rattler, its head and tail overhanging the station platform as its body gorged itself on passengers, I gorged myself on epic-length novels: *Kristin Lavransdatter*, klackety-klack, *Vanity Fair*, klackety-klack, *Jean Christophe*, *Buddenbrooks*, *Anna Karenina*. I barely heard the rattle, off as I was in Husaby, London, Paris, Hamburg, or St. Petersburg.

With the approach of spring, when the fires in the potbellied stoves in the waiting rooms were allowed to die out, the cars took on the animated air of European third-class railway carriages. The passengers exchanged greetings and fell into conversation. The men removed their jackets. There was no need to be furtive as I ate my peanut butter sandwich when pungent salamis and fragrant onion rolls were being consumed by my neighbors. Below us backyard gardens burst into bloom. Each day, during one of those inexplicable halts between stations, we were held suspended over one of them as if by design, to give us an eyeful of a flowering pear tree.

Windows in the cold-water flats that lined the route were thrown open with the first heat wave, drawing us into intimacy with the tenants. Tantalizing scenes flashed by — a husband and wife at the kitchen table, gesticulating at each other in anger, an adolescent girl preening herself before a mirror, a half-dressed couple making love — like movie stills with a jerky narrative, their only connective the identically shaped rooms, the exposed plumbing, the garish wallpaper. Plump-armed women, their elbows resting on window sills, stared back at us as if we, not they, were characters in a fast-moving drama. Life briefly became more absorbing than art. Only briefly. The husband and wife at the kitchen table were insufficiently dramatized to compete with Tolstoy's rendering of a quarrel between Anna and Vronsky.

Dr. Steiner lectured as did no one else at Hunter. He mused aloud about the authors and their works from his seemingly limitless store of knowledge as if he were talking to his peers. From time to time, remembering that we were students, he'd grab hold of the sides of his desk, lean toward us, and ask, Had we felt . . . ? Were we puzzled, as he had been, by . . . ? Didn't we think . . . ? Hmmmmmmm?

More often than not, I had not felt, had not been puzzled, had not thought as Dr. Steiner and probably the other students in class had done. I was doing the assignments all right, doing them eagerly, but my reading in this period resembled the performance of an unpracticed pianist whose playing is full of uneven tempi, false notes, slurred passages. Just as the pianist enjoys playing and is able to imagine how the music would sound if it were properly performed, so I reveled in these novels even though I suspected I was missing a great deal.

Riding the El again after class on the way up to Harlem, I reflected on what Dr. Steiner had said. Sometimes I suffered so acutely from an awareness of the inadequacy of my comprehension that I succumbed to the old feeling of hopelessness: I'd never, never catch up. To pull myself out of it, I'd remind myself how new the habit of reading was with me. I didn't read well, but I read. That was something, wasn't it? Hmmmmm, I'd say to myself, mimicking Dr. Steiner.

My literary life continued at the clinic. Because the money my father had left, which was to have seen me through college, had run out, I needed to supplement my income. Through a classmate who worked at the clinic I found a job there. Between registering patients and filing charts, my friend Helen and I discussed Literature and Life. It was she who introduced me to Proust, to T. S. Eliot, and to *Partisan Review*. After we closed the clinic for the night, we traveled home on the El together, talking about *The Sweet Cheat Gone* and the Albertine strategy. If we were deep in discussion when my stop came, she'd get off with me, we'd find an all-night cafeteria and continue talking over a cup of coffee. When I fell into bed, tired from the long day, my mind continued to spin: Anna, Vronsky, Arpad Steiner, Swann, Albertine, klackety-klack, klackety-klack into sleep.

As commencement approached, our thoughts turned from books to jobs. At least initially those of us with a B.A. degree would be no better off than high school graduates. We would have to learn to type in a hurry and scramble for the few openings we saw listed every morning in the want ads. (There were no openings for high school teachers of economics, and no sign there would be any in the near future.) In the final weeks there was no nostalgic singing of college songs, no yearning to extend the so-called carefree student days. We were impatient to move on to adult life.

No one was more eager to shake off the tyranny of term papers and examinations than I. Yet something told me that my education was not over. I could not have guessed that it was just beginning.

Chapter IX

. . . and that spelling. A little word "clean" comes out three different ways on the same sheet of paper. You know, as in "Mr. Clean"? — two out of three times it begins with the letter *K* as in "Joseph K." Not to mention "dear" as in the salutation of a letter: de–re. Or d–e–i–r. And that very first time (this I love) d–i–r . . . I mean, I just have to ask myself what am I doing having an affair with a woman nearly thirty years old who spells "dear" with three letters!

Alexander Portnoy in *Portnoy's Complaint,*
by Philip Roth

Van Zam Brothers, a real estate office opened by recent arrivals from Holland, offered me a job as a receptionist at the going salary for inexperienced office workers. Having looked at what was available to a college graduate who could almost type, as I almost could after a six-week course, I saw that I had no choice but to accept it. Young David Van Zam, who interviewed me, admitted candidly that there would be no way for me to use my knowledge of economics. Nonetheless, he wanted someone with my education because, as would soon become apparent, the job required great tact, and tact, presumably, was learned in college.

It was my duty to greet brokers — Europeans mostly, as one could tell at once from their foreign tailoring and floral eaux-de-cologne — and show them into one of three waiting rooms, depending upon how they fitted into a complex class system that had been worked out in Amsterdam and ill-suited New York. How to coax Mr. X into steerage, which is where he had been assigned in Mr. Van Zam's red leather book, when he felt he belonged in first class? "Tact, tact, tact," Mr. Van Zam counseled me was the way to do it. (The system would have to be overthrown, the Hunter graduate decided after the first week, if not by revolutionary methods then by the slower process of tactful re-education.) When not ruffling or unruffling feathers, I typed long incomprehensible letters in Dutch, which did little for my speed and gave me the dizzying feeling that I had my fingers on the wrong keys.

After five o'clock, when life began, I wandered around Greenwich Village looking for a room I would be able to afford when I received my first raise. When it came, it was not

easy to break away. Auntie, whose view of me had changed
little with the passing years, continued to think of me as
feckless and predicted disaster. My room would be disor-
derly; I wouldn't get to work on time; I would be too lazy to
study for the civil service examination for economists and
would remain an office worker forever. Lacking common
sense and good judgment, I would stay out all night dancing,
go without rubbers in the rain, come down with pneumonia
and . . . What would I do if I got sick? Did I ever think of
that?

Until the day I moved into a dark little room that gave on
the back garden of Alfredo's, an ex-speakeasy, I can't say that
I did. But after I had unpacked my clothes and had arranged
my Modern Library books on the table, the euphoria I'd been
feeling in anticipation of the move evaporated. Sitting on
the bed (there was no chair), my arms hugging my legs, my
knees tucked under my chin, I contracted into a tight little
knot of gloom. What had made me think I could manage on
my own? What, indeed, if I got sick? With not a penny in the
bank, a salary that would require careful budgeting to cover
my expenses, no resource to fall back upon (in those days
before health insurance), what would I do?

What had really brought on the blue funk — the question I
had never put to myself before, the question I now tried to
bury under a blanket of lesser concerns — was: Would I
make something of my life now that I, and only I, was responsible for my actions? Or would I slip into the quagmire
of sloth?

For hours I sat paralyzed by inertia. I heard the other
tenants come in after work, heard the muffled sound of their
feet as they climbed the carpeted stairs to their rooms. "Re-
spectable older men," they were, the landlady had said.
"Widowers mostly. They're quiet, leave the bathroom neat,
give no trouble, pay the rent on time." (The air of the house
was masculine and elderly — not the ideal place for a young

woman, but it was the only house with a room I could afford.) I heard the widowers turn the radios on softly for the
evening news, heard them wash up and go out for dinner,
felt hunger grow, told myself that I too must go out, and still
couldn't move.

So I sat in an agitated torpor — for how long? Perhaps as
long as it takes a snake to shed its skin. The colored lights
coming on in Alfredo's garden reminded me that this was an
evening not for brooding but for rejoicing. To celebrate my
independence, I would have dinner by myself and go to see
Benoit-Levy's *Ballerina* at the Art Cinema on Eighth Street.

At Ticino's, a basement restaurant with sawdust on the
floor, a literary clientele, and prices a third of Alfredo's,
Luigi, who had a soft spot in his heart for working girls,
heaped my plate with pasta, brought me a basket of Italian
bread, and filled my wine glass to the brim. After the movie,
the strains of Chopin running through my head, I strolled
through Washington Square Park in the balmy May air — no
hurry, no more curfews — across Eighth Street and up Sixth
Avenue to my new address.

Although Auntie and I had moved downtown to an apartment off lower Fifth Avenue just before I began to work for
Van Zam Brothers, I count the beginning of my Village life
from the day I moved to a room of my own on a raffish street
the other side of Sixth Avenue. The crisis I suffered on
moving-in day marked the death and burial of my youth, the
birth of my new life, and a determination "to show them."

After I had democratized Van Zam Brothers, I moved on to
a better paying job which permitted me to rent a larger,
lighter room in the same brownstone, furnished with a chair,
a desk, a small bookcase, and, most luxurious of all, a reading light over the bed. I hung a Degas reproduction on the
wall and filled the bookcase with second-hand books I
bought in the neighborhood on Saturday afternoons. Grateful to have a job that made my new life possible, I tolerated

the monotony of the work and continued for a long time to feel liberated when, at five o'clock, I was free to do what I liked with my evenings, without the nagging concern about preparation for the following day that I associated with a student's life. I delighted in my room, I delighted in my freedom to come and go as I pleased. While I stayed out late at night dancing, and never wore rubbers, I was in other ways so well-organized and dependable, and my room was so orderly, that those who had not known me growing up would have thought absurd my moving-in day fears that on my own, with no one to force discipline upon me, I would revert to the lazy, careless, untidy girl I had been in fourth grade.

Delight as I did in my new life, I nevertheless felt an unfocused yearning that was intensified every Friday when my landlady left with my mail a copy of the low-keyed, neighborly newspaper, *The Villager.* On Patchin Place, Minetta Lane, MacDougal Alley, according to its social news, there were literary teas and cocktail parties at which, I imagined, a roomful of Arpad Steiners sat around discussing Literature. Had I been able to arrange my life to perfection, I would have danced off both my shoes at the Stork Club one night, and gone to Patchin Place to listen to the literati on the other. There was Marie to discuss books with when I visited her on Long Island, and there were my women friends from college whom I met for lunch. But when I tried to talk about a novel I was reading with the young men I was going out with, I was actually accused of being a bluestocking!

Such an accusation would be unlikely from the instructor at Harvard I had met at a party the previous winter. He had come into the crowded room — a black-and-yellow muffler, as long as he was tall, wrapped around his throat, eyeglasses, high cheekbones, the slim build of a runner — obviously ill at ease among strangers. In the few minutes we had together I tried to make conversation. The muffler?

From Clare College, Cambridge. He had been a Kellett Fellow from Columbia.

Beneath the muffler, rather surprisingly, was a jaunty bow tie. There was nothing literary about our brief exchange (how to distinguish the two Cambridges was our subject), but I knew that John Berryman wrote verse and was poetry editor of *The Nation*.

Six months later, when he was back in New York for the summer, he asked me to go dancing. It had been my experience that the bespectacled, spelling-bee–winning brains I'd always been attracted to, the Arnie Rothsteins and Ray Taras, did not dance, so this invitation was as surprising as the bow tie had been. At the New Yorker roof, where Tommy Dorsey was playing, John crooned his French translation of "Night and Day" in my ear, and led me through set after set with demon dips and dervish whirls. Halfway through the evening I caught on. This was the performance of an ex-prom trotter who was mocking an amusement he had outgrown. It was true, John admitted. During his two years in England, he'd lost his taste for dancing. If it was a serious partner I wanted, I would have to look elsewhere. On the other hand, I knew by the time he saw me to my door that in his company I would not hunger for an invitation to Patchin Place.

Had I, at this time, met a man like Philip Roth's Alexander Portnoy, the romance would have been short-lived, and my progress toward literacy would have suffered a check so severe I doubt that I could have recovered from it. My case was more complicated than The Monkey's (Roth's character, whose spelling so shocks Alexander). Unlike her I had not the excuse that I was uneducated. I had been to college, and among my dancing companions even passed for bookish. Nevertheless my written English could, on occasion, be as ludicrous as hers. To my only correspondent with a critical eye, Auntie (who was now retired and living in New Jersey), I wrote stilted little notes taking care to substitute synonyms for words whose spelling I was unsure of. But if I wrote hurriedly, or when tired or preoccupied, I was capable of regressing to my P.S. 52 level, and yes, even of misspelling "dear."

How could I let a man as passionate about the written word as was John fall in love with me without telling him about my early difficulties, my patchy education, my continuing struggle? When I first tried to tell him these things, he wouldn't listen. He, too, was badly educated, he said. He hadn't studied Greek; his knowledge of German was rudimentary.

I shook my head: He didn't understand.

He, too, had wasted his years at Columbia. As a sophomore he had behaved so irresponsibly — cutting classes for weeks at a time, or appearing late for them still dressed in white tie and tails from a dance, failing to submit term papers or sit for exams — that he had been suspended for a semester and had had to convince the dean of a profound change of attitude before he was readmitted and his scholarship reinstated.

This mild confession I listened to in gloomy silence. Clearly he didn't understand at all what I was trying to tell him. He might not have done so for some time longer had I not gone to Long Island for a week to visit Marie and her family. Yes, yes, yes, I would write, I promised as I boarded the train.

The train hadn't picked up speed before I regretted my promise. I hated writing letters. I never could think of anything to put down on paper. And even if I could, would I want to risk addressing it to one who taught English A at Harvard? Might he not correct it in red pencil and return it the way Auntie had done with my thank-you notes? Each day, seeing John more and more as an English instructor and less and less as the man I was falling in love with, I found reasons for procrastinating. I delayed and delayed. I made one attempt. Tore it up. Made a second. Crumpled it into a ball. I agonized throughout the week the way I had done over freshman themes at Hunter. At the eleventh hour, I scribbled a note and put it into the mailbox.

In Penn Station, where John met me on my return, he led me over to a bench in the waiting room, looking as grave as a doctor who has read the X rays and must confront the patient with the bad news. "You thought you'd scare me off with this, did you?" He took the note from his pocket. "I must admit that at first it took my breath away. Then I saw it for what it is, not a love letter but a test of affection. Tell me about it."

He held the letter for me to see. My pale memory is that it looked something like this:

> Deare
> Time for olny a hurried note. M. and children well. Swimiming every day despite gary skies. Tomorrow we calabrent M's birthday. See you Thursday.
> > In haste,
> > Love
> > E.

Ashamed, repelled, for one wild moment I thought of denying that I had written it. I snatched the note from John's hand and tore it up. I knew how to spell "celebrate." And as for "deare"! If this was a test it was a severe one. I told John again what I had tried to tell him before. It was an abridged version of my academic history, but all the facts were there — the failure to learn to read in elementary school, the continuing difficulty with keeping letters and digits in their proper order, the inability to read aloud. This time he listened.

"It's as I suspected," he said. "Yours is not the functional illiteracy of the night school students I had when I taught at Wayne University. Your errors are not ordinary spelling errors. Hasn't anyone told you you have dyslexia?"

Braced for ridicule, it was a moment before I felt the well-ing-up of pure joy. My affliction *had a name!* To get hold of it, I repeated it: "Lysdexia."

John laughed. "There it is. A perfect example. You've scrambled the letters. It's *dyslexia*. A psychologist named Orton published a book about it in the late twenties."

I was stunned. What was wrong with me was a known en-tity, a psychological disorder. In a tumult of feelings, joy and astonishment were followed by outrage. If the book was pub-lished in the twenties, how was it no one in my family, none of my teachers had heard of it?

Orton's *Reading, Writing and Speech Problems in Children* was not published until 1937 (what John must have heard of was his 1925 paper " 'Word' Blindness in School Children"). Between the appearance of the article and the book, Orton had been doing research and developing remedial techniques at New York Neurological Institute, with grants from the Rockefeller Foundation. Because there continued to be so much disagreement about what constitutes dyslexia and what causes it, it was another decade before educators began to recognize the syndrome.

John said he had heard of dyslexia for the first time the previous semester. A brilliant student in one of his sections wrote papers so full of bizarre spelling that John had taken them to the guidance office to see what the psychologist could make of them. It happened that an Orton-trained re-medial teacher had just joined the staff. He was currently working with the student. John said that in the fall I must go to see this man, find out what he could do for me.

At first I was excited by the idea of being tutored, but the more I thought about it the more apprehensive I became. The word *remedial* filled me with dread. I associated it with plaster casts, braces, and crutches, and suspected that the tutor would be a Miss Henderson in disguise. He would treat me as if I were a defective child, bully me into reading aloud, and give me spelling words to write a hundred times. Underlying these fears was the conviction that it was too late: I was too old for reading training to be effective. (On all counts, I was wrong. Those who teach adult dyslexics are aware that their students come to them with just such preconceptions. The methods they use are essentially the same as those used with children, with the difference that the materials are carefully selected to interest adults and to take account of their general intelligence. The earlier training is begun the better, but it is never too late. What is required for success is a high degree of motivation on the part of the student and skill and tact on the part of the teacher.)

So when, early in the fall semester, I heard that the dyslexia expert had been drafted into the army, instead of seeing this as a lost opportunity, I was secretly relieved. And was even more relieved that by the time John and I were married, a year later, he had forgotten that I needed tutoring. What made it possible for him to forget is that never again did I send him a shocker like the test-letter. When I wrote him, I took the kind of care I'd taken with term papers. Instead of easier-to-spell synonyms I looked up the words I wanted in the dictionary. I made myself proofread what I'd written, hoping to catch scrambled words and omitted phrases. Whenever possible I typed. I was not a good typist, but my level of literacy rose when I typed. The speed of the machine, moving more nearly with the rhythm of my thoughts than a pokey pen, and the use of both hands, removing the old left/right conflict, reduced my errors.

In the beginning, supposing that what would interest John was "intellectual" letters, I wrote, say about an article in *Hound and Horn* he'd given me to read, and I had ill-digested, by the critic R. P. Blackmur. John might well have complained that he already had more than enough themes to read. Instead he said how entertained he was when I wrote about people. Abandoning Blackmur et al., I worked at being entertaining. At a party, at the theater, on a picnic, I found myself sketching how I would put what was happening on paper so that it would interest my reader on Beacon Hill who told me he was so greedy for my letters he raced down the stairs at the sound of the mailman's whistle. And by return mail, I received letters I read over and over again for content, learning, without realizing it, what no textbook could have taught me about style.

As the fat girl who has been nagged for years to lose weight slims down, as if by magic, once she falls in love, so I began to write letters that were light years away from anything I'd written before. And had the dyslexia expert still been at Harvard, and seen what I'd written, he would have said, mistakenly, that I was cured.

Harvard reawakened memories of the summer in Hanover. The years at Hunter, where the reality of college life had been so different from my girlish daydreams, may in part explain the excitement and awe I felt the first time John took me through the Yard. Because we lived in Boston, and I worked there, I never had quite enough of Cambridge. I looked for excuses to meet John on the steps of Widener, at Seaver, or in his office at musty old Warren House. My affection for the Yard spilled over into the Square, to the Coop, the restaurants and beer joints frequented by students, the bookshops.

Bookshops were one of our main forms of entertainment that year. When we wanted an outing and had little money (as was mostly the case, English A salaries being what they were), we'd go to second-hand bookstores to browse. Or rather I browsed. John combed the shelves, looking to fill the gaps of his extensive library. An extravagant man in other ways, he knew the value of each book and would not pay a penny more than he thought it was worth.

At home the education that had begun after the evening at

the New Yorker roof continued. If I say that John was my teacher, the most important I would have, I am likely to be misunderstood. The brilliant, witty, conscientious, intuitive instructor he was in class, I knew from the way he prepared, the way he talked about his students, the way they talked about him to me. The pedagogic role he played with me was more subtle. Had he been aggressively didactic, I would almost certainly have rebelled against his tutelage. Instead he allowed me to learn, in the way I was most capable of learning, osmotically. It was there, in the air, for me to take in as I was willing and able. The only direct recommendation he ever made was about what I should read.

"You hate Hardy, do you? I suppose they ruined him for you in high school. Try *Jude*. You'll see."

I saw.

"*Crime and Punishment* should be read in one sitting."

In an all-night, eye-aching session I read it.

"Prefaces to novels should be read not at the beginning but at the end."

I read them at the end.

Henry James was best read in a certain order.

That was the order I followed.

"You don't know Trollope? I envy you beginning him. Here. Read *The Eustace Diamonds*. I warn you, you'll become addicted."

(Never: "What? You *don't know* so and so?")

"Read this." "Read this." "Read this," he said, reaching down volume after volume from the shelves of the book-lined apartment into which I had moved.

Having found the perfect library and an unshockable librarian, I read and read, gulping down one novel after the other, eager to make up for lost time.

Had I attempted to read poetry, I would have been reminded how hard reading could still be for me. But John didn't recommend it, preferring to read it to me. That year he was writing a play about the Irish rebellion. Late at night, when he wanted a break, we'd go for a walk. Up and down Beacon Hill, he'd sing out Yeats:

> MacDonagh and MacBride
> And Connolly and Pearse
> Now and in time to be,
> Wherever green is worn,
> Are changed, changed utterly:
> A terrible beauty is born.

One might expect that it would have been more difficult for me to pass in academic society, especially at Harvard, than with my New York friends. And so it might have been but for the war which had greatly curtailed entertaining. There were none of those little dinner parties, such as I would go to later, where the guests behave as if they are examiners at Ph.D. orals ("What do you think of . . . ?" "Have you read . . . ?"), where one is expected to shine, compete, perform. Apart from an occasional cocktail party at the glamorous Mark Schorers, or those given by the students at Dunster or Lowell House, we went out little except, on Saturday evenings, to see Gertrude and Delmore Schwartz. With the Schwartzes I felt immediately at home, for as Delmore said, he was my "landsman." Not only had he and Gertrude lived on Washington Heights, up the hill from Inwood; they had also both gone to George Washington High School. Never mind that in their days there they had been writing poetry and publishing it in the literary magazines, while in mine I had been politicking. In alien territory, which Cambridge never ceased to be to Delmore, this gave us a bond.

Evenings at their apartment on Ellery Street were the high spot of our social life. Were ever two men as passionate about literature as were Delmore and John in those days? So different they were — Delmore, heavy set, with a large, almost handsome face (he described as "half Dimitri, half

Ivan"), gregarious, already famous, and thought to be the star of his generation; John, slim, fine-drawn, intense, coming out of a period of reclusiveness that had followed his return from England, little published and less known — so different they were and yet so much in agreement about what was Great, what was Interesting, what was Beneath Contempt.

No evening was complete unless one or the other read aloud, Delmore's delivery soft-voiced, almost conversational, John's highly inflected and dramatic. Unfailingly they read poetry — their masters', their contemporaries', their own. Sometimes part of a controversial article in the current *Partisan*. Or, Delmore's current obsession, a passage on psychoanalysis by Freud or Horney.

In a hilarious mood — and in those days when both men were full of great hope and grand ambitions and were free of the torments that would later shake their lives, the mood was often hilarious — John would read a story by Ring Lardner, act out a playlet by Chekhov, recite limericks and clerihews, or Delmore would take from his file (cardboard boxes from the grocery store) a sensational story he'd clipped from the tabloids.

A graduate student in English or a budding writer might have suffered at not being able to keep up with two such brilliant talkers. For me there was no question of keeping up. During those memorable evenings, I didn't talk, I listened, dazzled by the erudition and wit of the performers.

It was when we entertained John's students, and especially the four or five gifted ones who came to the house regularly, that I was more likely to suffer. It was when I was with them that I realized how much of what they were learning I had already forgotten. Freshmen though they were, they were already so much better educated than I that I often wondered if my attempts to make up for lost time weren't hopeless. I'm sure they (who had not only read all of Yeats, Pound, and Eliot, but were only a step behind Delmore in being up on the gossip about them) didn't guess it, but I was as much a student that year as they were. And I learned an important lesson. If I didn't want to make myself miserable, I must not compete with where they, or others, were, but with where I had been a year, three months, two weeks earlier.

Separated from my circle of women friends and the distractions of New York, I had another period of enforced introversion which gave me more time to read and listen than I would ever have again. By the time we left Boston in June, not only John, but I, too, had forgotten that I was dyslexic. That word, which I had been so overjoyed to learn existed two years earlier, I seemed unable to get a grip on — was it spelled *lys? lxy? dsy?* — and so it faded from my vocabulary. With the enormous gain in self-confidence that came from finding I could use my brain in a way that one had to use it in John's company, the painful early memories that had been vividly revived by my "deare-olny-calabrent" note also faded. I was ready to pass in academia.

Chapter X

I am still very ashamed of my inability to read. I
carry this dreadful secret always. I live in fear of having to read aloud something. At all costs I must con-
ceal my ignorance — a habit which dates from my
childhood . . .

"X," the dyslexic Englishwoman

In Princeton, where we went to live the following year, R. P. Blackmur stepped out of the pages of *Hound and Horn* to greet us at the station. Behind the courtly manner, the trim mustache, the tweedy professorial façade was a wild poet. So Delmore had said and had documented with countless stories. The only sign of this hidden personality I could see that first day was the rakish angle at which Richard wore his fedora.

As he walked us up through McCosh to Nassau Hall and Chancellor Green, down Prospect Avenue, where we would live for the next ten years, the Technicolor beauty of the autumnal day was given a dreamlike quality by the men and women dressed in turn-of-the-century costumes and riding around in horse-drawn carriages. They were not performers in a spectacle the University was staging to welcome us, as Richard puckishly suggested, but extras in a movie MGM was shooting of the life of Woodrow Wilson.

Since John taught intermittently after the first year, and then in the Creative Writing program rather than in the English Department, with no ambition to climb the academic ladder, I escaped the teas, committees, favor currying that I heard other faculty wives complain of, and was yet free to enjoy life in the kind of college town I'd fallen in love with in Hanover.

The year began not in January but with the opening of the fall semester. From one day to another, Prospect Avenue, which had been deserted during the summer, came alive with bicycle traffic. On my way home from work, I saw the football team practicing under klieg lights. If we were not at the game (we might well be, for John was a fan), the roar of the crowd at the stadium sounded in our living room like waves breaking on the shore. In October the concerts and public lectures at Alexander Hall began, and soon afterward Richard's Saturday evenings "at home."

Richard's evenings followed the pattern of Saturdays at Delmore's. Again the talk was literary. Delmore's verbal fireworks were replaced by Richard's stream-of-consciousness style, a style which gave one the feeling of eavesdropping on an interior monologue. He might go on for half an hour or more, seemingly talking to himself, and then suddenly say in a conversational tone, "You know John, your old friend Dosty knew a thing or two about . . ." And this would lead to an animated exchange between the two men about Dostoyevsky.

Or interrupting his soliloquy on Molly Bloom's soliloquy, he would point a finger at me and ask, "Why do women . . . ?" expecting me to explain the mysterious behavior of the members of my sex.

Since Richard's questions were whimsical, when they were not rhetorical, inviting me to speculate with him rather than testing my knowledge, I gradually became a participant as well as a listener. By the time the group doubled in size, as it did at the end of the war with the return of faculty members who had been overseas — after which the talk was as likely to be academic gossip as literature — I was completely at ease. Richard and John apart, I was as articulate as the others.

So comfortably did I pass in Princeton that I was unprepared for the crisis, as severe as the one I had suffered upon entering public school, that was on the horizon. A game, a seemingly harmless game, triggered it. We had gone to Cape Cod for vacation. After dinner one evening, it was suggested that we play "Ghost." The suggestion was greeted by the others, most of them writers, with enthusiasm. By me, with a feeble "Oh no!" "Ghost," depending as it did on spelling, was decidedly not my kind of game. It was not a game at all but a disguised pedagogical technique. Auntie had tried to use it once or twice, without success, in the sign-reading days. If I could now spell well enough with the help of a dictionary, and with pen and paper to permit me to make trials, without these crutches I felt extremely shaky. This evening, in a roomful of comparative strangers, there was no way out: They insisted I join the play.

As each one in the circle added a letter to build toward a word, I became aware that I was trembling. I was in P.S. 52, standing in front of the fourth grade classroom. Miss Henderson shouted, *"Wrong! Wrong!"* and called on the class to correct my error. The children's voices echoed through the years. In the summer cottage, the echo mingled with the roar of laughter when my neighbor narrowly missed disqualifying himself by adding a letter that would have made a word.

It was my turn. I gave the first letter that came into my head: "a." My neighbor on the other side behaved as if I'd chosen wisely. He built on my letter. In minutes the game would come full circle; it would be my turn again. Miss Henderson had found a new form of humiliation. She had sent me to a statewide spelling bee. The other participants, all winners in their schools, were seated around me. When I tried to explain that a terrible mistake had been made, that I didn't belong there, they wouldn't listen. The way to get them to listen was to give an absurd letter: "z." What could I possibly have in mind? My neighbor challenged me. I was out of the game.

Had there been just the game of "Ghost," I might have remembered the evening as merely an uncomfortable episode such as a nondancer suffers when he's dragged to his feet and made to perform in front of others. But a few nights later, when the same group was assembled, and "Ghost" was again suggested, there was a counter-suggestion that we read a play aloud.

Spelling and now reading aloud! What were amusements for the others, who had learned to read precociously and had been the stars of their classes, was torture for me. There could have been no more brutal reminder that I was far from cured. Had I been permitted to be an audience, as I was when Delmore, Richard, and John read, nothing could have pleased me more than to listen. To be asked to take a part set off the trembling again. Trying to keep the terror out of my voice, I declined.

I was sure?

Quite sure.

I was let off with the threat that I might be needed for the second act.

Shakespeare's lines were lost on me. I was back at George Washington trying to convince the advisor that I couldn't read at the assembly. Nonsense, she said. All I had to do was read, not act. I stood at the lectern, looking at the selection from the Bible. The page undulated before my eyes. Afraid of fainting, I gripped the lectern.

If only I *could* faint. Or bolt. If I ran out of the house and down to the beach, no one would be able to find me.

The second act had so many characters. Wouldn't I take a part now?

I was back at Hunter. A friend had talked me into going with her to audition for the Drama Club, which was to put on a play for the college at the end of the semester. I thought it a larky idea until, as the candidates were called to the stage, I realized what an audition entailed. One was not assigned a part to learn and asked to return in a day or two for the reading. One had to *sight*-read. How had I been so unthinking as to have risked exposure in this way? Feeling trapped, I thought only of escape. When my turn came, I shunted Mary into my place, and while she was reading, crept out of the darkened auditorium. Later, to excuse my behavior to her, I claimed stage fright.

It would be absurd to claim stage fright in the informal reading when the summer vacationers pressed me, so I limply begged off. No, I assured them, it wasn't a question of wanting to be coaxed. I really didn't enjoy reading aloud.

Not enjoy reading aloud? They were incredulous. Well, if I was sure . . .

I had escaped, but not unscarred.

Feelings of intellectual inferiority, which had been buried alive, and resurrected, could not easily be buried again. John had so completely forgotten my test-letter, and his diagnosis of my disorder, that he was baffled by my reaction to the vacation entertainments and to my fractured self-confidence. Trying to make him understand, I repeated the much-abridged history of my difficulties I'd given him in Pennsylvania Station. Because it was a subject I could not speak about without cringing, my account was diffident and undramatic, so undramatic that it had as little force as a svelte woman's account of what it had been like for her to grow up fat. She was slim now; that's what one saw. To imagine her otherwise was impossible. It was only she who carried around the vivid image of her former silhouette.

"What happened in Miss Henderson's class and in high school is *ancient history*," John said, his voice rising characteristically on the italics. "You certainly can spell well enough to play the game, and are equally capable of reading aloud. It's not like you to be so irrational. Don't you see that it's fear that keeps you from joining in?"

That it was irrational didn't make it less fearsome.

"If it had been with Delmore or Richard we had played the game you would have joined in, wouldn't you?"

I didn't know. I might have. They would have been less

shocked by my errors, or at least I thought they would have been. It wasn't simply that they knew me better, or that they had already made their judgment of my intelligence. Each of them had a well-concealed area of intellectual insecurity, as I had discovered, which I thought would have made them more sympathetic with my deficiencies. Delmore disguised his uncertainty about how to pronounce some words (words he'd heard pronounced one way at home, another way in school) by slowing down or speeding up his flow of speech. Once, reading a draft of a poem to John, he said the word "insane" with the emphasis on the first syllable. John, surprised, asked why. "Oh, you know me, John," Delmore said, making a joke of his error, "I say anything I can get away with." I heard the laugh, but felt the wince.

Of another order was Richard's insecurity. An autodidact who had never been to college, he had, despite his erudition, brilliance, and reputation as a distinguished critic, moments of uneasiness living in a society of Ph.D.'s.

Something told me the game-players in Wellfleet had no such feelings.

John asked if I wouldn't think it absurd, were there a psychologist on the Princeton faculty, to have remedial training now.

True, I was beyond that.

Did it not reassure me about my intellectual ability that he asked my opinion of what he wrote, that he valued my criticism?

Perhaps it should have done, but it didn't.

And what if I occasionally made a spelling error? Or stumbled over a line of Shakespeare? Yeats couldn't spell worth a pin, and probably couldn't read aloud either.

Briefly I was comforted. If Yeats couldn't spell either, I was in excellent company. I took a volume of his poems from the shelf. Not a single spelling error. They had been edited out of course, but I didn't think of that. Not finding verification, I suspected that what John meant was that Yeats had occasionally misspelled a word as anyone might do through inattention.

It was not in the poems but in Yeats's *Autobiographies* that I should have looked. There, in a few pages — one wishes there were more — he tells of his family's concern about his intelligence because he couldn't learn to read, and of his painful education under his father's tutelage. What is curious is that when I first read *Autobiographies*, the year John and I lived in Boston, I did not have a shock of recognition. It was only recently, rereading it, that I was electrified: Yeats was clearly dyslexic.

Reassurance such as John offered did little to buttress my self-confidence. Haunted by the past that I had tried so hard to forget, I began to wallow in self-pity. Why hadn't my affliction been diagnosed early? Why hadn't I been given remedial training? Auntie, Miss Henderson, the Model School teachers were to blame. I had had an inferior education at George Washington and Hunter.

Remembering that others had had excellent educations at both institutions, I took to flagellating myself: Why had I wasted hours daydreaming? Why had I squandered time aping Ginger Rogers when I should have been bent over my books? Why had I depended on others to do my homework? Why had I copied, cribbed, cheated, instead of doing the work myself, lazy, slovenly, frivolous girl that I had been?

It did not occur to me that it was not too late to compensate for my deficiencies and make up for lost time, until one winter day at the Institute for Advanced Study when I sat looking out of the window at the falling snow. At the time I was working there as a researcher for two economists who were writing a book to be called *Rebuilding the World Economy*. One of them had asked me to go to the third floor office where calculating machines were kept, to check statistics for a table they were compiling. The machine, in the perverse way machines have, had broken down. After an unsuccessful attempt to repair it, I sat wondering, dully, what to do next. The gently rising field between Fuld Hall, where I was, and the Director's house was lightly powdered with snow. As I watched the snowflakes, whirled this way and that by the wind, I asked myself: What am I doing here? Why am I working at this job?

Since my first days in Princeton I had worked at the Institute in one capacity or another. There could have been no more agreeable environment. The building and grounds had the tranquil atmosphere of a campus on which the faculty has remained to work after the students have gone away on vacation. At lunch and tea time the staff mingled with the scholars — the outstanding physicists, mathematicians, archaeologists, and historians in the country. From my desk each morning I saw Einstein, hair flying in the wind, sockless feet in moccasins, striding down the path to his office two doors away.

What I had not admitted to myself until this moment was that economics no longer interested me. What did interest me, what occupied my thoughts more and more, what Marie (who was now living in New York again) and I often speculated about when we were together, was the mystery of human motivation. As a child, buffeted by the moods of adults, I had thought that once I was grown up I would understand their behavior. Now, surrounded by even more subtle and complex personalities than those that had puzzled me in childhood, the mystery had deepened. Psychoanalysis, according to Delmore, had the answers. When I wasn't reading fiction, it was psychoanalytic literature I read for pleasure — never, surprising as it may seem, with a curiosity to find out more about what ailed me. My disorder, which felt like a pesky, mechanical flaw, seemed uninteresting by comparison with the baroque symptoms and eccentricities of my literary friends.

Examining the way I spent my day, I realized that from nine to five I was a clockwatcher who lived off the peripheral entertainments the Institute had to offer. How fortunate were those who spent the day doing what interested them! To work at what interested me would require further education. Since my college days, whenever the thought of going to graduate school had crossed my mind, I'd banished it instantly; I could not face the drudgery. Now, looking out the window, it occurred to me — my thoughts whirling like the snowflakes — that if I were to study a subject I genuinely wanted to learn more about the grind might be tolerable. And was it not possible that directing my own education, with the chance it would give me to do well what I had done so poorly in college, might go far to restore my loss of confidence?

What to study? After exploring the possibilities, I decided I wanted to become a clinical psychologist. Nowadays women are encouraged to resume their education after an absence of some years from academic life. Graduate schools are hospitable, courses are arranged for their convenience, and credit is given them for "life experience." Such was not the case when I began to apply. Princeton, whose department of psychology was a ten-minute walk from where I lived, would permit a faculty wife to audit courses but would not give her credit toward a degree. That meant commuting to New York.

At New York University, an administrator told me that I could not have chosen a more inopportune time to apply. Because of the G.I. Bill of Rights, which paid a veteran's tuition, the psychology department was flooded with applications. Only "the cream of the crop" could be accepted. One look at the transcript of my college record, which had been at the bottom of the pile on his desk, showed that I was not in that category. "A failure in mathematics in freshman year.

What makes you think you're graduate material? And why are you applying in psychology when you did your undergraduate work in economics?"

My interests had changed. I wanted to become a psychotherapist.

"Everyone wants to be a psychotherapist," the administrator, an experimental psychologist, said scornfully. "That's where the glamor is these days. With a record like yours . . ."

In junior and senior years my record had improved markedly, I pointed out. Besides, time had passed. I had changed. Now that I knew what I wanted to do, I would be a conscientious student.

"Do you have the innate ability? That's what I wonder. In any case the question is academic since you haven't the necessary undergraduate credits in psychology." He stopped bouncing in his swivel chair and leaned toward me as if he were going to give me a hot tip. "You're married, aren't you? If you're so eager to study something, why don't you study something useful? Like cooking. Hahaha . . ."

Whatever he said to discourage me only fired my determination. I waited for the hahas to die down and asked what I would have to do to get the necessary credits.

"Find a college where you can take the equivalent of an undergraduate major."

And then?

"Then, if you get straight A's" — he fired off another volley of hahas — "we'll take you in."

In September I was admitted to Douglass College, the women's division of Rutgers University, two bus rides and an hour's journey from Princeton. I was prepared for my new life to be uncomfortable, to find that the buses broke down in cold weather, to spend long hours in the laboratory, to give up social life to prepare papers. What I was completely unprepared for was the discovery that merely wanting to be a good student wouldn't make me one. As I scrambled to re-learn how to do square roots for a course in statistics, as I struggled to make sense of Woodworth's turgid prose on the physiology of the inner ear, my shifty old habits returned to devil me. Instead of studying Woodworth, I found myself editing him. Or worse, I used the words before me as background for musings, the way many concert-goers use the music. An hour would have passed, I would have reached the end of the chapter through which my eyes had scudded over and I would have read not a word. The library became an allergen again where my body gave me no peace. I was alternatingly hungry, thirsty, sneezy, sleepy.

When I should have been reading an article on the behavior of rats, I'd wander, in the old delinquent way, over to the shelf of journals and become engrossed in the case history of the even more interesting behavior of a man who thought he was a rat.

A report that was ready to hand in, I misplaced among my papers. Or accidentally tore up.

A book necessary for class, I absent-mindedly left on the bus.

No sooner did I sit down at my desk in the evening than my eyes slid shut.

My memory for names was unreliable. In the past, when I had had more serious symptoms to worry about, like not being able to read or spell, I'd rationalized this memory defect by telling myself that I didn't remember names because they didn't interest me; faces did. Now I discovered that even if I wanted to, tried to, I couldn't remember them. What was the name of the man who had formulated the resonance theory of learning? I asked myself in the middle of a test. It was . . . I knew it perfectly well. What was the good of having learned it if my treacherous brain misfiled it? The test was almost over before I found it. It was Holmheltz. A minute more and it would have been too late for one who was going for an "A." And surely the name was not Holmheltz but Helmholtz, I thought, quickly correcting it as I was about to hand in my blue book.

During those early weeks at Douglass, I was like someone striding across a field whose feet are grabbed by prehensile weeds. The harder I tried to kick free, the more vigorously the weeds pulled me down. Struggling to my feet, I questioned the wisdom of my decision to go to graduate school. My colleagues at the Institute had thought it was madness. My friends, whose invitations I was turning down to stay home and study, told me I wouldn't last out the year. Ten times a day, when I thought how long, how tedious, how dangerous was the road from Douglass College to my goal, I was on the verge of dropping out. Why, now that I wanted to do well, *had* to do well, was I behaving in this incomprehensible way? Why was I sabotaging myself? *Why?*

When I came to the realization that I would wait in vain for an answer, and accepted that this is the way it would be, I found I could work around my limitations as a student and the traps I set for myself. To avoid being tripped up, I must stop striding. I would have to *slow down.* It was no good trying to read Woodworth at the rate at which I read novels. To force myself to slow down, and to focus my attention on the page, I read with a pencil in hand, marking important or difficult passages. Proper names, which I found myself skipping over as I had done off and on since *Little Women* days, I made myself write on a piece of paper. Even that was not enough with my kind of memory. I had also to say them out loud: Helmholtz. Helmholtz. Helmholtz.

Since my resistance to this way of working was very strong, I limited myself to fifteen-minute study periods, with short breaks for physical activity (countless trips to the water cooler and pencil sharpener) in between. Assignments requiring the greatest concentration, I prepared in the morning, the time of day when I'm at my liveliest and my brain works best. In the evening, an uncomfortable chair and a harsh overhead light helped control my eyelids. If I found myself nodding off, I'd study standing up, or pace the room.

This plodding, flat-footed way of working felt like a strait-jacket, but it worked. By midyear, I realized that compared with the urban and competitive atmosphere I had known at Hunter, Douglass College, where the students knitted argyle socks for their boyfriends during classes, was going to be far less difficult than I'd imagined. The real test, I began to see, would not be one of intelligence. It would be a test of humility. In Princeton I was a faculty wife. In New York I was the wife of a poet who was becoming known (although not in New Brunswick). At the Institute I had had a status of my own. At Douglass I was an undergraduate. As an undergraduate I had to submit to discipline (no cutting of classes) and abide by rules (no smoking). For one who had been impatient to become an adult, it was disagreeable to be treated like an adolescent again. Never mind, I said to myself, I was on my way: One day I would be a psychotherapist and have an office in Princeton.

In June I had the Douglass transcript sent to New York University. Confident of being admitted, I spent the hours after work that summer in a carrel at Firestone Library, reading in the *Collected Papers* of Freud (and marveling at his prose style). July and August went by with no reply from the graduate office. In mid-September, just before the beginning of the new term, I received a form letter of rejection: "Due to the unprecedented number of applications . . . etc., etc."

The next morning I stormed into the administrator's office. Having satisfied the requirements he'd imposed, I demanded to be admitted. He again waved the Hunter transcript under my nose, said that to have done well at Douglass was no guarantee that I would make the grade among the brilliant students, "the cream of the crop," they were admitting. His eye was caught by something he hadn't seen before. "Wait a minute. What's this? You had to take a course in remedial English?"

I started to deny it. Ah yes, Idiot English. But that was so long ago . . .

"Don't you realize that I'm doing you a service by turning you down? You are wrongheaded to persist when, even should you somehow complete the course work, you clearly will never be able to write a thesis if you have trouble with English."

What if he was right? The unearthing of Idiot English made me lose confidence. Remembering the past winter, the effort I'd made, I came to my senses. I demanded an interview with the head of the department. After a three-hour wait, and a ten-minute interview, during which he studied my transcript from Douglass and reviewed my earlier conversation with the administrator, I was admitted to the Graduate School of Arts and Sciences.

On the way home I was exultant, but after a few weeks in the arctic climate at University Place, where students behaved like contestants in a race for which there was but a single prize, the bold façade I'd presented to the head of the department crumbled. With no way to measure myself against the others now that there were no classroom discussions and grades depended solely upon the final examination and term papers, I imagined that the cream of the crop were writing papers on a publishable level, and that after nights of cramming, during which I was in my pre-examination narcolepsy, they would write brilliant finals. *What was I doing among them?*

Marie, who was finishing her B.A. at Hunter at night and was also studying psychology, thought of a way to answer the question once and for all. My success at Douglass I now deprecated in the way the administrator had done. Reassurance, as usual, proved useless. What I needed was objective evidence: an intelligence test. And if it was to be valid, I should have it now before I studied it at NYU, as I would the following semester. She, who was learning to administer the Wechsler-Bellevue Test and was looking for subjects to practice on, would give it to me.

In the years since then, have I ever tested a patient more apprehensive than I was the day I sat opposite my sister at a table in the testing laboratory at Hunter? Looking very professional and unsisterly, Marie clocked me with a stopwatch on timed tests, recorded my responses. She went through the battery of mental exercises — block designs, puzzles, general information, digit span, tests of visual attention and ability to deal with abstractions — directing, questioning, timing, noting.

In another of those lightning slides down to the black hole of childhood, I thought of Auntie's, Miss Henderson's, the family doctor's speculation about what was wrong with me: the unverbalized question, "Is she . . . ? Could she possibly be . . . retarded?" My brain aching, my pulse racing, my stomach shriveled in spasm, I wanted to cry out, Stop! Stop! I don't want "objective evidence."

From far away I heard the examiner giving the reassurance she had been instructed to give anxious subjects — "Good." "Take your time." "You can do it" — while the fiend's mouth up against my ear hissed, "You haven't the innate ability."

While the examiner calculated the IQ, I paced in the hall outside. Calling me in, she handed me the Wechsler booklet. "You see? The 95th percentile for the general population. The geniuses you're surrounded by in Princeton probably rate higher, but it's quite high enough for the NYU Graduate School of Arts and Sciences."

There is no way to overestimate the importance of this episode in my cure. Had I performed poorly, I suppose the experience would have been disastrous, for Marie had convinced me of the soundness of the test and I would have been hard put to rationalize a poor showing. But then Marie wouldn't have given it to me had she not been sure I would do well. For years thereafter I kept the Wechsler booklet. Whenever I felt shaky, as I did whenever I dared take another giant step, I took it out of the file to reassure myself. I packed it with my papers when I moved to New York, again when I moved to Paris, again when I returned. Writing these lines I looked for the booklet again and couldn't find it. It must have been that during one of my periodic cleanups I came across it and, deciding I no longer needed it, finally threw it out.

As at Douglass College what had been put to the test was not intelligence but humility, so at NYU the test was not of intelligence but endurance. Did I have the stamina for the obstacle course? Could I stick it to the finish line? Tuesdays I left my part-time job at the Registrar's office at Princeton, took the train to New York, ate a quick sandwich at Chock Full O'Nuts, attended classes from six until ten, stayed overnight with Marie, spent the following day at the 42nd Street library, the evening again until ten at NYU, after which I took the train home to Princeton. The other graduate students had schedules no less demanding. Our professors were equally harried. They arrived for class from a day of work at hospitals and clinics, threw their briefcases on the desk, collapsed into their chairs, and droned on for two hours, often in a rambling disorganized way, while we listened for the most part in sullen silence.

Zigmund Piotrowski, a trim, elegant Pole, taught the one course, on the Rorschach test, that I was eager to get to and reluctant to leave. He encouraged me when I proposed doing a Rorschach study of poets for my thesis. The poets who were my subjects — Richard and Delmore, Mark Van Doren, Allen Tate, Robert Lowell, Randall Jarrell, William Meredith, W. S. Merwin — were friends. William Carlos Williams, whom I also wanted to test, neither John nor I had ever met. Responding to my letter, Dr. Williams said that if I could make John quit his study the following Sunday to accompany me, Mrs. Williams would give us lunch and we could make a day of it. John, who was working against a deadline on his *Stephen Crane* and was not going out, couldn't resist this genial invitation. On the train up to Rutherford I fretted over how to ask this stranger questions about himself I needed to know for the study. John, who admitted he would have responded glacially to such an intrusion from a prying psychologist, fretted with me. By the time the train pulled into the station, he was no less apprehensive about meeting the famous poet than I was.

Dr. Williams, looking, with his little black bag and aged automobile in which he had just been making house calls, more the doctor than the poet, greeted us as if he'd known us for years. Driving to his house he began talking in an autobiographical vein, with no prompting on my part, about his recent heart attack, his sense of mortality, his practice, his writing habits. Throughout lunch he continued talking, continued as he and I mounted the stairs to his study, recommenced after a two-hour interruption, the time it took to administer the Rorschach, when we rejoined Mrs. Williams and John for tea, continued on the way to the station, and broke off regretfully as the train approached — "There's *so much* I haven't told you!" — when, having embraced us, he waved good-bye, leaving John and me, who were now both in love with this ebullient, witty, "adorable" (John's word) man, to laugh all the way home about our needless concern on the way up. As John pointed out, after a day with my subject, I had only slightly less biographical data than he had on Crane after two years of research.

Collecting material for my thesis was more interesting and entertaining than it had any right to be, although there was a difficulty that a subject like Dr. Williams caused me. While I had learned to take notes reasonably well in class, especially with professors whose delivery was full of pauses and uhruhs, there was no keeping up with the voluble poets. What I had to do was transcribe my notes as soon as the testing session was over (in the case of Dr. Williams on the train back to Princeton) filling in the blanks from memory, and correcting the primitive spelling.

Once the protocols were collected, the serious trouble began. I was left alone, with a typewriter and a dictionary, to face the first extended piece of writing that had ever been required of me. The thesis was the most difficult, the most painful, and the most useful requirement I had to fulfill for my degree. It taught me that I could not write when I felt like writing, for I never felt like writing, but must work every day. It taught me that what I first put down on paper could only be brought up to an acceptable level if I was willing to stick with it through quadruple the number of drafts a student without my disability would have found necessary. It taught me that the periods of frustration, discouragement, and even despair I suffered — when, throwing the unyielding dictionary at the wall and pounding my fists on the ungenerous typewriter which gave back only what was put into it, I was about to give up — were transitory and built into whatever I would try to do.

John, who was now working against the ultimate deadline on the Crane, took time to read my thesis the night before I submitted it. His generous praise told me I had nothing to fear from the committee of professors that would judge it. Bracing myself I asked, "And the spelling?"

"You probably should spell 'colour' without the 'u.' "

Ah yes. A new complication in my difficulties with spelling was that I unwittingly copied John's British usage. While he used it uniformly (and his editors indulged him in the practice), I used it haphazardly — one time spelling the word "color," another time, perhaps on the same page, spelling it with a "u." On the train to New York, I raced through the manuscript, Americanizing the spelling. A month later, I was awarded my degree.

What had made the long haul through graduate school tolerable was that on the nights I stayed in the city, after class I would walk through Washington Square Park to meet Marie who was studying for her master's at the New School. Going home on the subway, before going to bed, in the morning after her children had gone off to school, in the reading room at the 42nd Street library, we talked and argued and clowned about psychology. During those two years we recaptured the intimacy we had known growing up. Then we separated again, she to take up a fellowship at Vanderbilt University for her Ph.D., and I to begin an internship.

Chapter XI

Not the eye but the brain learns to read.

Reading Disabilities, by Knud Hermann

It has always been a grief to me not being able to read aloud to my daughter, from her childhood upwards. I often tried.

"X," the dyslexic Englishwoman

In a continuing effort to control my education, I resisted the strong pressure one felt in graduate school to go on for a Ph.D. and set out, in those anarchic days when the training necessary to become a clinical psychologist and psychotherapist was less clearly delineated than it is today, to find an internship. The director of the Rutgers Psychological Clinic, the formidable Dr. Anna Starr, a physical and intellectual giantess, offered me an opportunity to work with children referred from all over the state who fell into a broad range of diagnostic categories. She promised to teach me what she had learned during her forty years as a clinician in return for my sharing with her a back-breaking caseload. I hesitated about accepting because I had hoped to specialize in the treatment of adults. In the end she convinced me that a woman going into private practice, as I told her I planned to do, would have a far better chance of building up a clientele if she was willing to begin by taking children.

It seemed ironic that my first assignment was to test the boys and, more rarely, girls who came to the Clinic because they could not learn to read. It was up to me to discover whether their failure was the result of limited intelligence, emotional problems, or dyslexia. Dyslexia was the category about which I was most ignorant. It had not been covered in any of my courses, and when, out of curiosity about myself, I had tried to find out more about it at Douglass or NYU, I had found that after reading a page or two of an article I had become so queasy that I had had to give up. Did this carsick feeling (for that's what it was like) come from a reluctance to revive painful memories? I wondered. Certainly my feelings about the whole subject were complex. I never mentioned to anyone that I was dyslexic (only Marie and John knew). For long periods I conveniently forgot that I was. And when I did remember, I both wanted and didn't want to know more about it. Whatever the reason for the liverish feeling, I had no choice but to push past it now if I wanted to understand the patients Dr. Starr was asking me to test.

As I quickly discovered, the literature on what causes dyslexia is voluminous, contradictory, and inconclusive. Having to read it proved to be the ultimate test of reading comprehension for me. There were passages I was forced to go over five and six times before I could get even a slippery grasp on their meaning. (Between my old habit of scudding down a page, eyes glazed over, and my somatic discomfort, it was hard going indeed.) This was partly because neurologists and psychologists often don't agree on terminology, nor even about what symptoms should be included in the disorder. What they do agree about is that in the act of reading the eye picks up the stimuli — letters, words, numbers — and transmits them to the brain. So it is to the brain, that infinitely complex and mysterious organ, that one must look for an explanation of why dyslexics behave as they do.

The brain is divided into a right and a left side. The two sides, called hemispheres, are connected by a bundle of nerve fibers, the corpus callosum. By what seems an unfortunate complication of neuroanatomy to those, like me, who have difficulty keeping right and left straight (and here my queasiness begins), the brain is cross-wired to the body: The right hemisphere controls the left side — arm, leg, etc.; the left hemisphere controls the right.

At birth infants are ambidextrous. By the time they reach school age, 90 percent show a preference for using the right hand. From this it can be inferred that they have become left-brained; or, to put it another way, the left has become the dominant hemisphere. Of the remaining 10 percent, some are left-handed and therefore right-brained. Others remain ambidextrous, which means that neither hemisphere has taken over the dominant role.

At approximately the same age, the activities of the two hemispheres become specialized in another important way. Language, which earlier was processed by both hemispheres, comes under the control of the left hemisphere for all but one percent of right-handers and all but 30 percent of left-handers. For the majority, then, the reading hemisphere is the left; for the minority, the right. So much in simplified terms for what is known.

Now for what is hypothesized. Orton was struck by how many of the nonreaders he saw were ambidextrous, or left-handed, or had mixed dominance (right-handed but left-eyed, -eared, -footed, or any of the possible combinations). It seemed to him that a delay in establishing dominance for handedness reflected a delay in establishing a dominant language hemisphere. Instead of the left hemisphere being in control (or, in the minority, the right), it was sometimes the left, sometimes the right. Hemispheric activity was competitive rather than synchronized. The result — confusion, reversals, twisted symbols.

Orton's hypotheses were hotly disputed by neurologists. In England, under the direction of Macdonald Critchley, in Germany, Scandinavia, Czechoslovakia, and France, as well as in other research centers in the United States, those who studied the murky question of causation came up with conflicting findings. Some thought the whole question of handedness and mixed dominance (about which many papers were published following Orton's work) was a red herring and were vexed at the attention given to it, attention they felt could more profitably be expended searching elsewhere. Others hypothesized a delayed development of the fat-like myelin sheath that insulates and protects nerve fibers as the cause of dyslexia. Or a focal maldevelopment in the parietal lobe of the brain. Or a defect in the overall organization of cerebral functioning. Or a maturational lag. Or a combination of all of these.

For fifty years the battle about causation has raged. Recently at the UCLA Brain Research Institute, an experiment using computers to analyze the EEGs (electroencephalograms) of dyslexics showed that in their brains the activity between the two hemispheres is less synchronized than in the brains of the control group, which has added a certain weight to Orton's theory. With the invention of new equipment like the Caltech optical device, which permits scientists to observe cortical activity, and with the extensive research now being conducted on patients who have undergone split-brain operations, it is possible that the mystery of what causes dyslexia will be solved in the near future.

Psychoanalysts who have been interested in dyslexia have taken a different point of view from that of the neurologists. According to psychoanalytic theory (which I was able to read without physical discomfort), reading is a way of sublimating aggressive drives. The inability to learn to read is a neurotic symptom which stems from strong unconscious and unsublimated hostility toward a parent. As a three-year-old refuses to eat to punish his mother, so the seven-year-old refuses to learn to read. Analysts do not say, as is sometimes claimed, that all cases of reading disability are the result of neurosis: rather, that perhaps 20 percent are. And that this 20 percent, whose disorder is primarily psychological rather than physiological (and who are therefore not, properly speaking, dyslexics), need psychotherapy before they can benefit from remedial training.

Orton, who was a psychologist as well as a neurologist, was not unaware that the children referred to him often had emotional problems. He believed that for the most part they were the result of the disorder, not the cause. Dyslexic children arrived at school as well-adjusted as their classmates. As the others began to learn the basic skills on which the rest of their education would depend, they, whose brains sent them confused messages and to whom a page of print was in a code to which they could not find the key, were failing the most important test of their academic careers. Their parents and teachers told them they were careless, inattentive, and lazy, that they had the ability to learn if only they would try. Since as far as they could see, they were not careless, were attentive, and were trying, these wide-of-the-mark criticisms compounded their confusion. Before long they developed a profound sense of intellectual inferiority and an aversion to the classroom, to books, and to learning that could not easily be eradicated. All this in contrast to precocious readers who developed a sense of intellectual superiority and self-confidence that would remain with them throughout their schooling.

It did not surprise me to learn that the seat of the disorder is in the brain. In my own case I had localized it there at age nine. (I had even felt, or believed I had felt, a *brain*ache, which is quite different from a headache.) The jamming, blocking, and confusion I suffered from I had likened to a mechanical breakdown — an out-of-order switchboard, two typewriter keys locking so that neither prints. As for that red herring, handedness, I was a clear-cut example of mixed dominance: left-handed, -eared, and -eyed at birth, right-handed by training. In periods when I had looked for a scapegoat to blame my failures on, I had blamed my first grade teacher for changing my writing hand. It was disconcerting to discover that my left-handed nephew, whose writing hand had also been changed, showed not a trace of dyslexia; whereas my niece's son who is dyslexic in the same degree as I and with identical symptoms to mine is an unchanged left-hander.

It did surprise me to learn, however, that boys are affected three to four times more frequently than girls. When this statistic began to appear in journal articles, its validity was questioned. Did it only seem that boys were more susceptible because, until recently, parents and teachers were more concerned with their education than with the education of girls? Or was it that girl dyslexics were "good" in class, whereas boy dyslexics were disruptive, calling attention to their academic failures? Though the reason for the 3:1 or 4:1 ratio continues to be the subject of speculation, it is now considered valid. It is also found among stutterers and is seen by many as another indication of the natural physiological superiority of women, a superiority which accounts for their being longer-lived than men.

As Orton continued his research and examined more and more nonreaders, he realized that it was a mistake to associate handedness patterns with reading disabilities in any simplistic way. What was of prime importance, whatever the cause of the disorder, was remediation. With this Dr. Starr wholeheartedly agreed. Her concern, as she told me, was not with theories. It was with what could be done for the nonreaders who were referred to the Rutgers Clinic by the schools.

At the end of each term the Clinic telephone rang unceasingly. Frantic parents begged for the earliest possible appointment. They had been summoned to the school and warned that their child was failing and would not be promoted because he didn't know how to read. Frightened and angry, the parents had demanded to know why, since the child was in third grade (or seventh or eighth if it was a girl, and a "good" girl), they had not been told before. *What was to be done?* The school advisor, trying to calm them down, had said that if they were willing to see a psychologist . . .

By the time Dr. Starr saw them fear and anger had intensified. And the child they brought with them, who had lost two or more years of language training, was either passive and fatalistic ("I'm a dumbbell and will fail no matter how

hard I try") or aggressive and defiant ("I hate school and nobody is going to make me study").

Dr. Starr assigned me the task of preparing the psychological reports on the children. Screening them for defective
vision and hearing, administering an intelligence test
(which, unlike those they'd been given in school, required no
reading), as well as personality and achievement tests, I was
struck by the low view they had of themselves. When my
year of internship was over and I became Dr. Starr's assistant, it was I who interpreted the report to them. Remembering how helpful the objective evidence of the Wechsler
had been to me, I went over the results with them in detail,
told them what they had done well in, what poorly; told
them they were bright, very bright, or had superior intelligence, whatever the case.

In order to correct the children's misconceptions about
their disability, I asked them first to tell me what they
thought explained their failure. Then, in terms they were
able to understand, I corrected their misconceptions, with an
explanation of what dyslexia is, tailored to their age and intelligence. And to be sure they had understood, I asked them
to repeat the explanation in their own words. Since they had
often come to the Clinic full of apprehension about whether
they were retarded, or "bad," they were relieved and reassured. From experience I knew this reassurance would be
helpful only temporarily. The ones with a deep-seated conviction that they didn't have "a high IQ" would need to be
reminded of the test results from time to time (as I reminded
myself by looking at the booklet of the Wechsler Marie had
given me). I knew, and told them, that in the long run the
only thing that would convince them of their intelligence
and increase their self-confidence was success in learning to
read. At the Reading Center, where they would go twice a
week, they would be given remedial training. There was no
disguising what they would do there as fun and games. It

would be slow, hard work. They would often become discouraged, but if they persevered, they would learn to read.

Toward the end of my two-year assistantship, Dr. Starr, forgetting my plan to go into private practice, began grooming me to replace her when she retired. It was an inheritance I fought shy of, not least because it would have required me to supervise the Reading Center. One might have predicted that a history such as mine would have been ideal preparation for helping those similarly afflicted. It is true that I was quick to diagnose dyslexics and enjoyed testing them. Their training I had to leave to others, for merely to enter the room where they were struggling over their workbook or chanting their exercises made me feel low-spirited, even oppressed. And while it soon became clear to me that I had the makings of a psychotherapist, it was equally clear to me, if not to Dr. Starr, that I was insufficiently objective with the pupils at the Center to be useful, much less happy, working with them. (Other dyslexics, who don't feel as I did, often make gifted remedial teachers.)

When Dr. Starr pressed me to stay on at the end of my appointment, I confessed my feelings about the Center and offered my case history, much abridged, in explanation. She was incredulous. What nonsense! I could never have been like the children at the Center. To pretend that I had been was "self-dramatization." Perhaps I had been a little slower in reading than in other subjects . . . but dyslexic? Impossible.

Dr. Starr, who never saw adult dyslexics, or rather, didn't recognize them because they passed so cunningly, underestimated what they are capable of, even without remedial training (as witness the list of those who have become famous). One way or another, intelligent dyslexics do learn to read — inefficiently, painfully, slowly. What proper teaching spares those who receive it is the inefficiency, a good deal of the pain, and the terrible waste of years.

After three years at Rutgers, I went into private practice with a psychiatrist who opened an office in Princeton. As Dr. Starr had predicted, in the beginning my referrals were mostly children. Among them was a small proportion of dyslexics. Although I still was unwilling to confess to others that I was one (and would have been disbelieved had I done so), I told the children who came to me for testing, and their parents, that I, too, had had a reading disability. It seemed to me that the parents took even greater comfort from my admission than did the children. Having coaxed, bribed, bullied, and punished the child to no avail, they had so lowered their aspirations for him that they wondered if he would ever be capable of earning a living.

Eager to do anything they could to get the child to read, the parents asked how they could be helpful at home. Since by the time I saw them the nightly lessons had deteriorated into shouting and crying scenes, I recommended that they leave the actual training to the remedial teacher to whom I was referring them. What they could do at home was read aloud. To a boy of nine? Of eleven? Wouldn't it keep the child from reading on his own? Wasn't it a form of indulgence? No and no. As the child began to learn to decode, they could begin books for him that were on his reading level, take over briefly again when he got bogged down, turning it back to him again. But this alone was no substitute for reading aloud. And as for whether this was not a form of babying or indulgence, I reminded them that until the advent of the radio, reading aloud had been a source of pleasure and entertainment to people of all ages. Only recently had it been relegated to the nursery.

It didn't take me long to see that for my recommendation

to be effective, parents had to enjoy reading aloud. If it bored them, or if they themselves read poorly, it was better to find a substitute, an older brother or sister, or even a neighbor. This is especially true of the dyslexic parent, like the anonymous woman "X," for whom reading aloud remains painful. Other dyslexics find that with an eager and uncritical child as audience, they are finally able to overcome their inhibition. So it was with me. When Marie's children begged me for a bedtime story, I couldn't resist. It is thanks to them that I finally made my way down the list of classics — *Black Beauty, The Adventures of Tom Sawyer, Treasure Island*, and the other books the Inwood librarian had urged on me and I had returned unread.

As my practice grew, I once again commuted to New York, this time for weekly sessions with a training analyst who supervised the psychotherapy I was doing. Dr. Anna Katz agreed to take me on if I would undergo a personal analysis. If this was essential for one who wished to be a psychotherapist, as she said it was, I was willing to comply, although on my own it would not have occurred to me to be analyzed. Having resolved the crisis that had sent me to graduate school, I could not imagine what, apart from my relations with my patients, I would have to talk about, for I was novice enough to believe that one had to have "interesting" tics, phobias, obsessions, and compulsions in order to interest a therapist.

Certainly I did not imagine the day I walked into the darkened room that what was to begin as an intellectual exercise would have effects so profound I would be feeling their vibrations to this day. During those hours of discomfort, bafflement, anxiety, astonishment, and exhilaration on the couch I learned, among so many other things, that while I had come a long way since the afternoon I'd sat looking out at the snow from the Institute window, I could go a great deal further. My horizon was limited not by the mechanical difficulties caused by dyslexia, real though they were, but by the old myths about me that I had incorporated. The answer to the why? why? why's? I'd asked myself at Douglass, when my behavior as a student had been incomprehensible to me, was that the role of "dullard" held no surprises, whereas the role of "brain" was full of hidden terrors. What had felt like prehensile weeds tripping me up was the child I had been, tugging at me in fear, holding me back.

When John was invited to the University of Cincinnati to take the Elliston Chair of Poetry for a semester, I had occasion to test this insight. Through the courtesy of the University medical school, I was permitted to participate in ward rounds and staff conferences with doctors doing their residency in psychiatry and neurology. The dull-witted, delinquent child I had been, whose behavior I now recognized for what it was when I tore up important notes, misplaced textbooks, and fell asleep in the University's medical library, I had to learn to live with. She had not died the day I moved into my room in the Village, as I'd thought she had. I would never be able to shake her. When she tugged at my leg, begging me to play the dodo, it was no good (though it was unavoidable) to become impatient. What I had to do in order to keep going was to pick her up and run with her, reassuring her that there was nothing to be afraid of.

As my eyes began to close over my library book, I would say to myself: You're not sleepy but afraid. When I accidentally tore up my notes, I would say: You are not careless but afraid. Having recognized that fear was the enemy, I had to fight it. Cincinnati was a battleground. Every day there was a skirmish. How many of them I'd won, I didn't realize until I returned to Princeton and took up my practice, which now included adults as well as children, with heightened self-confidence.

*

If I were asked to put my finger on the moment when I was willing to consider myself cured, I would say it was the day I received a letter accepting the first paper I sent to a professional journal. An article in the *American Psychologist*, taking private practitioners to task for not subjecting themselves to the discipline of writing papers (a discipline imposed on academic psychologists who must publish to be promoted), stimulated me to organize the thoughts I had had for some time on a modification of a personality test I thought might be useful to other clinicians. I worked on my paper evenings and weekends (since the breakup of my marriage the previous year, I had been looking for an engrossing activity to fill my free time) and sent off my modest effort with a timid hope and a self-addressed stamped envelope. Ten months later I received a letter from the editor. He was sorry to have delayed so long in answering. He had procrastinated because he had not known how to tell me that, hoping to make a final decision on a stack of manuscripts while on vacation, he had taken mine to Cape Cod — where it had been swept off his desk and out to sea in a hurricane! Suspecting, correctly, that I had no copies of the patients' drawings that had accompanied it, upon which my argument depended, he apologized profusely.

He was not to blame for what was clearly an act of God, but when I finished my next article, I selected a journal in the Middle West, well out of the hurricane belt, and was more successful. The day I received the acceptance letter, I did a little dance of joy. When the offprints arrived, I took one to Auntie. If she had been pleased about my having earned an advanced degree, or about my professional success, she had never shown it. About the article she was frankly delighted. It was not that she would read it (it could not have interested her). It was that I had given her concrete evidence to show that her pushing and goading had been to some purpose.

On the drive back to Princeton after the visit, I realized it was not the *American Psychologist* that had nudged me into writing the article. It was the need, never satisfied in the days of my high school and college political and social triumphs, to coax out of Auntie — the most important of "them" I had vowed to show — the approval she had until now withheld.

In the last years of Auntie's life, it fell to me to look after her affairs. As her health failed, it became clear that she would have to live where she could be looked after. After a long search, the only place I turned up that I knew she would find tolerable was an oasis of tranquility, of trees and lawns, of doctors and attendants, not far from Theodore Roosevelt High School in the Bronx where I had done my practice teaching.

On my visits to the home and, after Auntie fractured her hip, to the hospital associated with it, I once again traveled the route familiar from my college days. In the intervening years the Third Avenue El had lost miles of its track and all of its jauntiness. Gone were the rich aromas of Middle-European kitchens. The new passengers did not eat in public, although a few disreputable men drank surreptitiously from bottles hidden in brown paper bags. The tenants in apartments along the route were hidden from view now, their eyes turned inward on television screens. In the winter the car doors froze open. In summer they jammed closed. The elevated stations wobbled dangerously, unequal to the burden of the approaching train. More than once service broke down completely, forcing the passengers to find other means of transportation. The El had grown senile like many of the aged patients I saw on my visits to the hospital. My affection for it, sorely tried on these weekly trips, was based on my association of it with my first reading of *Anna Karenina* and the other books on Arpad Steiner's list.

Thinking back to the college girl who had read *Ulysses* behind the packing cases at Kline's Pharmacy, it occurred to me for the first time that Auntie had sent me to the lending library to select reading matter for her as a ruse, hoping, still, to stimulate my interest in books. How many other ruses had she tried, and failed with, before this one? She and I had never talked about my old difficulties, not even when I gave her my first article. When I broached the subject on one of my weekly visits to see her, Auntie behaved as if I'd committed an indiscretion. Each time I tried she changed the subject.

Only through an oblique reference could I refer to this part of our shared past. It vexed her mightily that at the age of 84 she sometimes couldn't recall a name she was looking for. Or that she said one word when she meant to say another: "salt" for "spoon." "What's the matter with me?" she'd ask, with a mixture of apprehension and impatience. "Am I becoming senile?" I could tease her into being more tolerant of the tricks her mind played on her by reminding her that if these lapses were a sign of senility I had been senile since childhood. At such times she'd look at me sharply. Then with an ambiguous gesture, and an "Oh you . . ." (meaning "Oh you . . . don't try to jolly me out of my exasperation with old age"? Or, "Oh you . . . you were a special case"?), signifying that she was at least momentarily comforted on that score, she would tell me about one of her other concerns — her fear of losing her eyesight or her battles with the physiotherapist who was trying to get her to walk.

Born the year the El was constructed, Auntie died the year it was dismantled, taking to the grave the answers to my questions. The unanswered questions, the lurching rides on the El to visit her, and the memories of the past those rides revived set in motion the train of thought that led to the writing of this book.

Chapter XII

When will such a prolific writer [Hans Christian Andersen], already quite well known in his native country, learn to write his mother tongue correctly?

C. Molbeck, a contemporary critic, reviewing Andersen's latest book, from *Hans Christian Andersen*, by Elias Bredsdorff

In early drafts, Virginia Woolf's practice regarding punctuation, spelling and capitalization was highly erratic . . . It was her practice to submit her work to her husband Leonard, for revision of these details, and he . . . did not hesitate, as he writes . . . "to punctuate" these essays and correct "obvious verbal mistakes" . . . The quality of the typing is poor even by Virginia Woolf's none too stringent standards; punctuation and spelling errors abound.

Editor's note by Jeanne Schulkind in *Moments of Being*, by Virginia Woolf

Since there is no cure for dyslexia, when I say that I was willing to think of myself as "cured" what I mean is not that I was, or am, symptom free, but that my symptoms are manageable — at least on good days.

On good days I spell reasonably well. Words I'm uncertain about I can find in the dictionary without difficulty. (It is on words I think I know how to spell that I'm likely to be tripped up. Throughout this manuscript I spelled "led," "lead.") I have not advanced so far that I would think of playing a word game, such as Scrabble, or my only nightmare, "Ghost," for pleasure. Spelling remains hard work — such hard work that I am an untrustworthy proofreader of my own copy (although, curiously, not a bad one of other people's).

When I speak there is no trace of the early confusion I sought to cover up by clowning. I say precisely what I mean to say.

My sense of direction is adequate for everyday use if I depend on feel rather than left/right, east/west. In a strange city, especially a complex European one, I get lost probably twice as often as other tourists. As a reader of maps, I leave much to be desired.

My memory, which has always been excellent in some areas, serves me well even where it is weakest: in the recall of proper names.

Employing digits, whether in conversation, dialing telephone numbers, or doing accounts, I make errors caused by transpositions less than a quarter of the time.

As for reading, it is one of my greatest pleasures — a pleasure blunted only by a feeling that I must hurry to make up for lost time. Even today, I occasionally look up from a page suffused with joy and wonderment and say to myself, *I'm reading!*

There is nothing I like better than to pass my time in reading rooms of libraries. Like other habitués, I have my favorites: the 42nd Street Public Library, where I spent so many hours during my years as a graduate student, The New York Academy of Medicine, and, the one I think of as my club, the New York Society Library. The only remnants of a finicky taste in books is my lack of appetite for detective stories and an aversion for fairy tales and fables. Just recently, Bruno Bettelheim's *The Uses of Enchantment* and my curiosity about Andersen's life and the way he reworked it into fiction have helped me to partly overcome this aversion.

Reading about dyslexia, or more broadly, neurology, remains difficult. When Marie, who is now a psychologist at a Boston hospital, sent me an article she had written, "Ideation in Patients with Unilateral or Bilateral Mid Line Brain Lesion," I again had to imagine wires from the right side of my head to my left hand and foot, and the left side of my head to my right hand and foot, fighting off, paragraph by paragraph, the inevitable motion sickness and tendency to get the wires crossed.

I have never learned to read and eat at the same time, as during a solitary meal I've wished I could do. Nor can I attend to two competing sounds — a voice and a radio, two people talking to me simultaneously — even on good days.

On bad days, which are brought on by fatigue, strong preoccupations, illness, and what else I don't know because I sometimes can't pinpoint the cause, I have little confidence in my ability to spell. The dictionary proves useless because I can't think of the opening letter or syllable that will help me find the word I want. I write down an approximation of the spelling, and the following day, if it's a good day, I can correct it with ease, wondering what could have caused me trouble.

Taking notes is as troublesome as it was in my freshman year in college. If the notes are important, I retype them as soon as I can, trying to unscramble them.

In conversation I say one thing when I mean to say another — "The car they sold him was a melon." "You can't pull the wool over my ears" — that sort of thing, and am usually unaware of having done so. What I am aware of is the blocking that, on occasion, makes it impossible for me to find a word I want. It feels as though two words surface and jam, prohibiting me from articulating either. (This is quite different from stuttering.)

On bad days my directional guide is so completely out-of-order that I walk blocks to the north when I want to go south. I am capable of overshooting the entrance to my apartment building, or even the door of my office.

My memory for proper names is so treacherous I have an acute awareness of what it must be like, at least in this regard, to be senile.

Numbers become scrambled so that I mis-dial, mis-address, and mis-calculate three quarters of the time. In conversation, I might say that Columbus discovered America in 1942, and wonder why people are amused.

In reading I have the old trouble with scudding. This morning when I was going through the motions of reading an article in the newspaper, I was actually planning how I would write this paragraph when I got to the typewriter, as I realized when I reached the last sentence of the article and hadn't the slightest idea what had preceded it. This warned me that today I would have to make an effort to fight off preoccupations that would give way easily enough to other intellectual activities, but not to reading.

If, on a bad day, I have to go to the library to do research, I am tormented by hunger, thirst, and drowsiness as in the old days. Instead of reading, say, about dyslexia, the purpose of my visit, I wander over to the shelves of periodicals and become immersed in the articles on the Vitamin C controversy.

Even on good days I can have a bad period during which I behave once again like a delinquent student or the family idiot. At such times it is not easy to sort out what behavior is the result of the disorder and what the emotional overlay. After working efficiently all day at my practice, a social gathering in the evening can trigger a bad period. It would be to a historian that I would more than likely make the error about Columbus, especially if he carried over his professorial manner into society and struck me as a pedant or quiz-giver. It would be at a literary gathering that I would be unable to remember the name of an author I know perfectly well. Impatient to get on with what I have in mind, I say, "The author is . . . a woman . . . graying hair . . . parted in the middle . . . drawn back in a bun. Not Virginia Woolf. Not Elizabeth Bowen. No, no, no, not Louise Bogan," baffling my interlocutor, who is not amused to have been drawn into a guessing game that eventually gives me the name I was looking for: Yes, of course, Doris Lessing.

Far and away the most disconcerting and vexing symptoms nowadays are the lapses of memory and of speech. These are the ones that take me by surprise and endanger my passing, because I have learned no defense for dealing with them. I suppose these failures give me the startled and perplexed look I've seen my dyslexic grandnephew, Billy, wear when he's telling me about an athlete whose career he's following closely, whose name is . . . ? He frowns in puzzlement, snaps his fingers. How could he have lost this name he knows so well? Unless he is more successful than I have been in finding a device to deal with these lapses, he is likely to suffer all his life from a symptom most people are happily free of until they reach old age.

With the publication of my first article, I thought that probably all I could look forward to, by way of further improvement, was for the proportion of good to bad days to increase. And slowly they did — from 10 to 1, to 20, and then 30 to 1, although usually with the bad days clustering together, two or three at a time. My story would have ended here had I not remarried and gone to live in France for four years. The first week in Paris I learned two things that turned my life upside down. The first was that it was illegal for me, a foreigner, to practice my profession; the second, that my tourist French would not serve me well enough to run a household, much less to converse in polite society. A tourist may speak "a little French." A resident is expected to speak it fluently, as my husband did, or remain silent. Unable to do the former, and unwilling to do the latter, I became a student again.

It is often said that dyslexics cannot learn a second language. Here, as elsewhere, I think their potential is underestimated. In two years of hard work I learned to speak and read French. The spelling I never mastered. If I had to communicate by letter, I wrote a rough draft and had Bob (a spelling bee winner in French as well as English, who proofreads everything of importance before I send it out) correct it.

After I felt sufficiently fluent, I proposed to a psychological journal (to which I had for some time been sending reviews of French books) that I write an article on the psychoanalytic milieu in Paris. For this project, the most ambitious I had undertaken since my thesis, I interviewed psychiatrists, analysts, educators, and for a year attended clinic meetings and supervisory sessions on a regular basis.

After sending off my paper, I was at loose ends for the first time since my arrival in Paris. More than one of the analysts I'd interviewed had suggested that I might, after all, be able to practice again. (When I raised the question of legality, one of them shrugged, "Ça alors . . ." If one were to pay attention to the law one would never accomplish anything.) What would be required was for me to see patients in controlled supervision, as I had done at the beginning of my career, this time under the supervision of a French psychotherapist. It being June, nothing could be decided until the fall — which left me with the summer to do the touristy things one never has time for once one gets caught up in the life of the city. I visited museums, went to the collections, sat in cafés, met Bob in the Tuileries for lunch.

In August, after the shopkeepers in the *quartier* lowered their metal shutters, the bakers whitewashed their windows, and the restaurateurs pulled down their shades for a midsummer slumber, I came to a full stop, the first full stop since the day I'd moved into my room in the Village. It was not an entirely comfortable feeling. One morning, as I was sitting in the garden, the newspaper on my lap, unread, my eye was caught by a mop being shaken out of an office window twenty yards away. It was the Spanish cleaning woman signaling me that she had not joined the exodus from the city. She had been my silent companion since Bob and I had moved into the apartment. I'd looked up from the unpacking to see her there across the way, leaning on her broom, observing me with frank curiosity. She had been there during the period of my lessons when, bored with my *devoir* in the textbook (*Est-ce à ou de?*), I had looked out of the window. She had been there later when, typing the article, I'd stood up to stretch my arms. We had often exchanged thoughtful, quizzical looks, wondering about each other's lives, so different, and yet not so. Being women, did we not have many of the same needs, desires, and fears?

An idea for a story about her occurred to me. An article,

perhaps . . . but a story? Before leaving New York I had made one attempt at writing which had had nothing to do with my profession. To help pass the time while Bob was off on a long business trip, I had written a travel article about a visit we'd made together to West Africa. A literary agent who saw it said, "Why don't you try writing fiction?"

He didn't know to whom he was talking. Had he suggested I try tightrope walking, I could not have found the idea more inappropriate, even alarming.

("*You* write fiction?")

I had completely forgotten Carl Brandt's suggestion until the moment the idea for the story occurred to me. Recalling it now, it made me feel as dizzy as if I had mounted a high platform and were looking down on bottomless space with nothing between me and it but a line of rope. To rid myself of the vertigo, I took up my newspaper. We were leaving for Lisbon in a few days, I told myself, so there was no point in beginning anything now, and when we returned it would be September, time to investigate more seriously the question of taking up my profession again.

The Spanish cleaning woman followed me to Portugal. When I saw she would give me no peace, I began writing, using hotel stationery. There followed a period of bad days as severe as any I'd suffered at Douglass. Superimposed upon the predictable difficulties that assail me when I even try anything new and ambitious was the confusion caused by my recent immersion in the French language. The new language had loosened my slippery grip on the old one. French idioms crowded out American usage. Verb tenses, which I had heretofore used by ear rather than by rule, were now governed by the French sequence of tenses. My spelling became a jumble of French and English, the English its usual mixture of American and British usage.

The strain of trying to write brought on a relapse. If I couldn't produce a simple declarative sentence, and there were days when I couldn't, how would I ever manage ten pages of fiction? I ran through the repertory of dirty tricks I'd played on myself whenever I'd tried to take a giant step — at Douglass, at NYU, in Cincinnati — sometimes despairing, sometimes watching my performance as one watches a clown on ice. Nevertheless, I was so absorbed in what I was doing that I persisted, and upon hearing that we would be going back to the United States at the end of the year, I abandoned the idea of working in my profession and continued writing.

Had my practice been awaiting me upon my return to New York, I probably would have become caught up in it and abandoned the novel I had begun on the long boat trip home. But after a hiatus of four years, I had to rebuild my practice. For months I agonized over what to do: Should I devote my time to seeing patients, work I loved and knew I was good at; or should I continue trying to write, with everything to learn and no guarantee that I would ever be successful? In the end I realized it need not be either/or. Why not both?

To get my hand in again (and work my way out of the cross-cultural shock that came from returning to the much changed America of the midsixties), I accepted a part-time job in a psychiatric clinic. The rest of my time I divided between my practice and writing.

If, after I published my first professional paper I had thought of myself as cured, the attempt to write fiction taught me that I would have to push past merely hoping for an increase of good over bad days. The way I read, which on good days at least I had thought of as satisfactory, would not do at all. I would have to force myself to read much more slowly, and with attention to the techniques the masters had used to produce their effects. Flaubert, Joyce, Henry James, Faulkner, I reread with new eyes. The new way was to the reading of the Boston days, when I had devoured the books on John's shelves, what the Boston days had been to the subway reading of the books on the list for Idiot English at Hunter.

When the first draft of my novel was finished, I realized that one of the most difficult things for a beginning writer is to find a critic. Because I had not told any of my friends, certainly none of my literary friends, what I was doing (how could I tell them when I had hardly admitted it to myself?), I felt reluctant to approach them now. So it was with some hesitancy that I asked the novelist Caroline Gordon, an old friend, if she would read the draft for me. A generous and exigent teacher, she showed me how much I had to learn, how much more work I had to do, and she encouraged me to continue. After another year of writing and rewriting, she said that the manuscript was ready to be sent out. It was rejected by the first editor to whom I sent it, lost for eight months by the second, and returned, unread, by the third, with the query: What have you had published?

I put the novel aside and began to write articles and short stories. Walter James Miller, who read and criticized the stories, encouraged me, when they began to be accepted, to take out the novel and rework it. After it was published, he invited me to be on his radio program, *Reader's Almanac.* Over the telephone I accepted and asked how I should prepare for the interview. No need to prepare, he said. He would ask me a few questions and have me read a section from the novel for discussion.

No sooner had I hung up than I began to tremble violently. "Read a section . . ." he had said.

(*"You* read aloud? And in public?")

Every day for the two weeks before the program, I was at the point of calling Walter, to beg off. What if I froze, as I had done at the freshman assembly in high school? I had read aloud to Marie's children, and to Bob, but to no one else. Still it wasn't the convoluted lines of Shakespeare or

Gerard Manley Hopkins I was being asked to read on the radio. It was what I had written and rewritten so many times I should be able to "read" from memory, as in the old days. But suppose memory tricked me into reading an earlier version . . . It was no good. I couldn't do it. And yet if I could . . .

I reminded myself that there are dyslexics who take a more rational attitude toward reading aloud. A poet and teacher, whom I had heard read verse in class, I had spotted as a dyslexic. Yes, he was one, he admitted, when I asked. His history was different from mine. His parents had had him tested when he was a child, had found that he had superior intelligence, and decided to ignore his inability to read, convinced that he would begin to do so when he was ready. They enlisted his teachers' cooperation so that he was never asked to read aloud and was never ridiculed for his poor spelling. Eventually he did learn, and by the time I met him he was an unusually penetrating and gifted reader not only of verse but also of philosophical and scientific writing. When I asked how he felt about reading aloud in class, he said it didn't trouble him in the least. He had long since accepted that he would make errors, as he had accepted that he would make errors in spelling, and thought it was of little importance. In no way did it affect his view of himself as a teacher or writer.

How sensible, I thought. And yet, there was no way I could adopt the same attitude. I went to the radio station as to my doom. Walter, who must have thought mine was the usual nervousness of the unpracticed performer, smiled encouragingly when I delayed after the signal to begin. I heard a hollow voice repeat familiar words. Afterward Bob told me no one could have guessed what I had been feeling. I would like to be able to say that when it was over I was exhilarated with an "I've done it!" feeling. The truth is that I paid such a heavy price for my effort in exhaustion the next day I wondered if it had been worth it. Was there no end to the struggle?

Only recently, while writing this book and working through the relapse brought on by it, did it occur to me that each new step is nothing more than a temporary resting place. A new dissatisfaction, coupled with a spurt of energy, will drive me on to yet another stage in the unending striving to be cured.

Chapter XIII

. . . some afternoons he ["Chris," a nine-year-old dyslexic] would come home from school in despair, hurl himself, sobbing, onto his bed, and say he wanted to throw himself out the window.

"The Last Skill Acquired," by Calvin Tomkins,
The New Yorker, September 13, 1963

My history is by no means ancient history. Although considerable progress has been made in the development of remedial techniques since Orton's time, the recognition of the elusive flaw proceeds slowly and unevenly.

There continues to be broad disagreement about what symptoms should be included in the syndrome and even about what to call it. (Aside from the tongue twister *strephosymbolia*, some forty names have been suggested.) This confusion is reflected in the statistics about its prevalence. As an official at the Department of Health, Education, and Welfare explained, "Developmental dyslexia is not yet a clear-cut diagnosis like stuttering. Some experts include brain-damaged children, for example, while others believe they belong in a separate group. Depending on who has defined the term and collected the data, as little as 5 percent and as much as 25 percent of the population is said to be affected." In the fall of 1978, Dr. Jan Frank and Dr. Harold N. Levinson, two psychiatrists at New York's Downstate Hospital who believe they have discovered yet another possible site for the neurological disorder — the cerebellum, the organ behind the brain stem — reported that they had found an incidence of 15 percent. But the figure most commonly quoted, the one given out by The Orton Society, and corroborated by other English-speaking countries, notably Canada and England, is that one person in ten is dyslexic.

The Orton Society, established in 1949 by June Orton, Dr. Orton's widow and colleague of many years, today has 20 branches in the United States. It has done more over the years than any other group to educate professionals and the general public through articles published regularly in its *Bulletin* and *Reprint Series*. The Society also organizes international conferences at which authorities from all over the world meet to exchange views. And yet at report card time clinic telephones continue to ring clamorously, with parents, who have been told their child is a nonreader and won't be promoted, pleading to be seen at the earliest possible moment.

It was not when I was a school girl decades ago but in the sixties that Chris's mother, Mrs. Palmer, called the Pediatric Language Disorder Clinic at Columbia-Presbyterian Medical Center, asking for a consultation. She had been told that her son was in need of immediate and intensive psychiatric help. Chris, the subject of Calvin Tomkins's 1963 article in *The New Yorker* (an article that elicited an unprecedented number of letters and requests for reprints), was nine years old and failing in the good suburban school he was attending. Beginning in first grade he had had trouble learning to read. His teacher recommended that Mrs. Palmer work with him at home. When Mrs. Palmer became frustrated, Mr. Palmer took over. These lessons ended predictably. Despite Chris's lack of progress, he was promoted. In second grade his resistance to reading and writing was "impenetrable." He also became moody and withdrawn and started having nightmares. At the end of the year, it was decided that he should repeat second grade and have extra help at school in reading two afternoons a week.

Being left back was a severe blow to Chris's pride. He began to have violent temper tantrums and talked of suicide. By the time he was seen at the Language Disorder Clinic, he was so out-of-control that he had thrown a stone at a classmate, inflicting a head wound that required seven stitches. Psychological testing revealed that Chris was severely dyslexic. With Mrs. Katrina de Hirsch as teacher-therapist, he was given intensive remedial training.

Prevention of academic failure through early recognition and intervention (remedial training) has lagged so far behind the knowledge now available that Tomkins ended his article on this gloomy note:

> At the moment, therefore, the outlook for children with dyslexia is fairly discouraging . . . Some of them, like Chris Palmer, will be lucky enough to get the right sort of help in time . . . The majority will go untreated, and will probably grow up believing that they are hopelessly dullwitted.

It was almost ten years later, in the seventies, that my niece, whose son was attending a highly respected private school in Boston, was told that Billy was failing and would have to repeat second grade. If we had not had him tested, and thus discovered that he was dyslexic, he might have continued to fail until he had become as despairing as Chris.

There are times, of course, when the school has been alert to the child's problem and it is the parents who have delayed taking action. They have been so frightened by being told that their child is a nonreader that they haven't heard, have refused to listen. More than one illiterate adult has brought suit against a school system, claiming that his disability went unrecognized, only to have the court rule that it was not the school that had been negligent, but the parents who had turned a deaf ear to the school's recommendations.

The spate of articles in the popular press in the last five years, in which, unfortunately, dyslexia has sometimes been used as a catchall term, has led many educators to react by denying that the syndrome exists at all. Today the situation is paradoxical. In some schools children are tested in kindergarten to screen those who are likely to develop reading disabilities. A vigorous remedial program may follow. Just as frequently what follows is an indifferent program or no program at all. In schools where the principal denies the existence of the syndrome, and the teachers have come from training schools and teachers' colleges where they have not been taught to recognize the symptoms, dyslexics have as little chance of being recognized as they had in the nineteenth century.

At the most recent International Conference of the Orton Society, in 1976, representatives from England, Germany, Holland, and Canada lamented the resistance of their own governments to recognize dyslexia and bemoaned the lack of progress in training special teachers. They looked somewhat wistfully at Czechoslovakia, where a model program has been set up which they would like to see duplicated at home. All children in Czechoslovakia are tested upon admission to school. Dyslexics are divided into four groups. The mildest cases go into a regular class and receive additional help from the classroom teacher. In the second group the child goes after school to a clinic for training with a remedial teacher. The mother accompanies her child so that she can cooperate in the program, working with the child at home in ten- or fifteen-minute sessions every evening. (Since with early intervention there is no history of failure on the child's part, or panic and anger on the parent's, the parent/child relationship has not been contaminated by misdirected efforts, and these sessions are effective.)

On the third level, children are separated at the beginning of their schooling and, unlike those in the two earlier groups, are put into special classes. These children, who would fail hopelessly in the regular program even with after-school help at a clinic, need special instruction in all subjects, not just reading, because of the severity of their disability. A "therapeutic attitude" on the part of the teacher, whose aim is to establish a "joyful atmosphere," insures that the child, and parents, don't develop feelings of inferiority about being in a special class.

Children with symptoms and concurrent emotional problems so severe they are not likely to respond even in special classes are placed in residential centers for a combination of psychotherapy and remedial training.

In a vast and democratic country like the United States such a program would be impossible to organize on a national level, because education is the province of the individual states, not the federal government, and school districts, and even principals, are often autonomous. Through the recent Education of the Handicapped Act, however, demonstration centers are being set up. In Shelburne, Vermont, for example, all preschool children are observed in a series of activities geared to the child's age level. If the early education expert from the state agency, to which federal funds have been given, agrees that the child is what is called "potentially learning disabled," a trained paraprofessional is sent into the home five hours a week to help parents improve the child's learning skills.

Since dyslexics are less obviously handicapped than other groups, there is some question about how large a slice of the federal pie they are likely to be given. In the end, whether preventive measures are taken depends on pressure from parent groups and on the schools. In schools with enlightened principals and generous budgets, programs that approximate the Czech system do exist. In others, there is the usual two- or three-year delay before tardy and far more expensive remedial training begins, often, as in Chris's case, with an overlay of emotional problems so severe that the special teacher has to assume the role of psychotherapist, at least for the first few months.

The gravest maladjustments occur among those in large classes in low-income neighborhoods who drift to high school on social promotions. These adolescents find their way not to reading clinics but to correctional institutions. Harold S. Danenhower, in his article "Teaching Adults with Specific Language Disability," says that 31 percent of teen-age nonreaders in a correctional institution that was studied were not retarded or functionally illiterate. They were dyslexic. While in upper-class families untreated dyslexics often become ne'er-do-wells and black sheep, among the "disadvantaged" they frequently become delinquents. The most chilling example cited of a man with above-average intelligence and a reading disability that went untreated is Lee Harvey Oswald.

Dr. Lloyd J. Thompson, a psychiatrist widely known for his work on dyslexia, says in an article published in 1964 that he made a tentative diagnosis of Oswald's dyslexia on the basis of newspaper articles about him that followed the Kennedy assassination. There wasn't time for his request to examine Oswald to be granted before the assassin was in turn assassinated. Later, when Oswald's Russian journal was reprinted in *Life*, Thompson was able to corroborate his hunch. The spelling errors, which had not been corrected, were typical not of functional illiterates but of dyslexics: giued (guide), Sovite (Soviet), wacth (watch), fonud (found), leauge (league). (Oswald may have faked the dating of the diary, as has recently been suggested, but this kind of misspelling would be hard to fake.) He also spelled the same word in different ways at different times. Long and difficult words he spelled correctly, while easier ones, learned at an earlier age, he misspelled. Thompson concludes,

> If Oswald did have dyslexia, as the evidence strongly indicates, the consequent years of education frustration from ages six to seventeen, without understanding on his part, or the part of others, might have been a fundamental factor in producing hostility and rebellion against society and the social order as represented by those in authority.

Many other factors in Oswald's life — the absence of a father, the role his mother played, the frequent changes of school — influenced his behavior, of course, as Thompson admits.

In striking contrast to the failures are the success stories of other undiagnosed and untreated dyslexics who not only overcame their disability but also became famous. While it is entertaining to speculate, as some experts do, about whether Demosthenes and Leonardo da Vinci were afflicted with the disorder, what is more useful is the examination of the lives of those who lived closer to our time and left sufficient evidence to justify the diagnosis. Woodrow Wilson was one such, according to his biographer, Arthur Link. How the boy who didn't learn to read until he was eleven developed what is probably the largest recorded vocabulary (6700 words) and an admirable prose style is well documented. Professor Link says that Wilson is particularly interesting to neurologists, one of whom is currently at work on a medical biography, because after he suffered a stroke that temporarily paralyzed his right arm, he began to write, and write beautifully, with his left. Since stroke victims ordinarily have to go through a tedious period of retraining before they are capable of making the change, Wilson's left-handed facility raises the question: Did he belong to that 10 percent of the population in whose brain the right is the dominant hemisphere?

Hans Christian Andersen has been studied by a Danish expert, Axel Rosendal. About his dyslexia there seems to be no question. It is startling, therefore, to read in his autobiography, *The Story of My Life*:

> From as early as I can remember, reading was my only and dearest occupation; my parents were poor, but my father was very fond of reading and therefore had some books, which I swallowed.

From what is known about Andersen's nightmarish difficulties in school, his lifelong inability to spell and to write his native language accurately, such precocity seems highly unlikely. What he probably remembers is wishing he could read, play-acting at reading, turning the pages of a book while daydreaming. (As a general rule, it is probably safe to say that anyone who confesses to having been retarded in reading can be believed; claims of precocity, especially where coupled with signs of a language disability, must be viewed with skepticism.)

Einstein was among those cited by Dr. Thompson in his article, "Language Disabilities in Men of Eminence." As a child Einstein was introverted, even withdrawn, and so slow to learn to speak that his parents wondered if he was abnormal. Although a rebellious student who hated learning by rote, at the age when Wilson was just beginning to read he was devouring popular books on the natural sciences (according to Max Talmay, a medical student who boarded with the Einstein family), and at thirteen read Immanuel Kant. In 1971 Ronald W. Clark, author of *Einstein: The Life and Times*, rejected the claim that he was dyslexic, calling it "understandable special pleading." Professor Gerald Holton, an Einstein authority at the Jefferson Physics Laboratory at Harvard, wrote, in answer to my inquiry, "While Einstein was slow to speak as a child, he was not slow to read. He sometimes made spelling errors in English, but not in his native language."

If Einstein should be dropped from the list, Flaubert and Yeats should be added. We know about Flaubert's difficulties in learning to read from the account left us by his niece, Caroline Commanville, and through Sartre's biography, *L'Idiot de la Famille*. Yeats is explicit about his early education in his autobiography. Denis Donoghue, the editor of Yeats's *Memoirs*, says of the later years, "As for spelling and punctuating, Yeats never mastered those skills."

Less certain, but worth further investigation, are two women candidates, both renowned writers, who are otherwise so different that they make an unlikely pair: Virginia Woolf and Agatha Christie. An examination of their manuscripts to see whether their spelling errors are characteristically dyslexic and additional information about their early years, especially the ages at which they learned to read and to write, would be needed before a definite diagnosis could be made.

The heavy emphasis on writers may seem surprising. There is no reason to believe that there are more dyslexics among them than, say, among painters and architects. But writers tend to write about their early relationship — whether happy or traumatic — to the written word and to books; whereas those whose talent is nonverbal either do not write autobiographies or, if they do, stress what in their early education was important for the development of their talent.

Nelson Rockefeller, the only living eminence usually mentioned, has not written an autobiography, but he has admitted to being a dyslexic on more than one occasion — usually when he has made one of those verbal slips which are so unnerving to dyslexics and so incomprehensible to others. His most extensive statement was written for a PBS television program on learning disabilities called "The Puzzle Children," and reprinted in the October 16, 1976, *TV Guide.* In it he talks about his dyslexia and the humiliation he suffered as a child because he could not read aloud. He says that even today reading aloud is so difficult for him that he has to have long words in his text broken into syllables and sentences broken into segments. Then, experienced as he is, he "may have to rehearse it six times."

Between the failures, like the institutionalized delinquents, and the outstanding successes, like Nelson Rockefeller, are the majority who pass unnoticed. "Gail," the subject of an article by Phyllis Steingard, "The Unheard Cry," was a 30-year-old woman when, through her sister who was taking an education course at Villanova University, she came to Mrs. Steingard's attention. After making the diagnosis, Mrs. Steingard asked Gail if, under the protection of a pseudonym, she would be willing to write about her experiences as a child. Here are excerpts from "Gail's" autobiographical fragment:

> I can't explain how I feel inside all my life I have been so humileated about school & so defeated in my academic efforts that until reading these books I could not dusscuss school in any aspect even with my husband . . .
>
> I had so many problems as a child at home & and in school that I hated life I hated mysilf I felt most of no all of my problems were phylologal . . . My family said I was a cold rock no feelings no nothing. I would never show emotion I was a pro at hiding my feelings I would not react in amy way to any situation I didn't laugh or cry until I was into my middle twentys. Sometimes I felt as though I would explode from within, I had so much hurt bottled up inside if only I could cry or scream . . .
>
> Sometime in elementary school about 4th or 5th grade I started putting a not [note] on all my papers in the corner
>
> $$HME$$
>
> I continued this message until 11th grade. I was repremanded over and over for doodling on the paper but no one ever ask me what it was, even though it was on all my work. I rote it by placing one letter on top of another open up it said HELP ME.

One cannot help wondering what this "super-sensitive, emotionally-scarred, brilliant woman," who on the intelligence test scored in the very superior range, would have made of her gifts had her cry, "HELP ME!" been heard.

Today identification of children who will develop a reading disability is possible at an early age. These children can, and should, be tested before they begin their schooling. Such testing is not expensive, nor does it require highly trained examiners. Identification is worthless, of course, unless followed by special training. With what is now known about the reading process, there is little excuse for allowing a child to fail in school, and possibly throughout life, because of dyslexia. Such a failure is not only the child's. It is also society's.

Acknowledgments and Resources

For Further Reading

Acknowledgments

I would like to thank Mrs. Elizabeth Travers, Director of the Educational Therapy Clinic of Princeton, for permitting me to observe the children and the teaching methods at the Clinic.

The Yaddo Corporation deserves and receives my thanks for its generous hospitality.

Resources

The International Dyslexia Association (formerly The Orton Dyslexia Society)
International Office:
8600 LaSalle Road
Chester Building, Suite 382
Baltimore, MD 21286-2044
Telephone: (410) 296-0232
or 1-800-ABCD123
Fax: (410) 321-5069
E-mail: info@interdys.org
Web site: http://www.interdys.com

Branches of the International Dyslexia Association

ARIZONA
Judy Zola, President
P.O. Box 6284
Scottsdale, AZ 85261-6284
(602) 941-0308

CALIFORNIA
Central California Branch
Kathy Nielsen, Contact
P.O. Box 223258
Carmel, CA 93922
(408) 659-7653

Inland Empire Branch
Betty Meeks, President
P.O. Box 6701
San Bernardino, CA 92412
(909) 686-9837

Los Angeles Branch
Donald Hoagland, President
4379 Tujunga Blvd.
Studio City, CA 91604
(818) 506-8866

Northern California Branch
Martha Renner, President
#4 Heritage Court
Atherton, CA 94027
(650) 328-7667

Orange County Branch
John W. Schroeder, Pres.
293 W. Cerritos Avenue
Anaheim, CA 92805
(714) 564-0777

San Diego Branch
Patricia Hensley, President
P.O. Box 87448
San Diego, CA 92138-7448
(619) 295-3722

CANADA
June Green, President
#820-470 Granville St.
Surrey, B.C. VC6 1V5
(604) 584-0564

COLORADO
Denise Ensslin, President
P.O. Box 102092
Denver, CO 80250
(303) 721-9425

D.C. CAPITAL AREA
Valerie Andersen and Julia Pascu, Co-Pres.
12201 Parkstream Terr.
Herndon, VA 22070
(703) 827-9019

FLORIDA
(FL, PR)
Barbara King, President
5005 Laurel
Suite 100
Tampa, FL 33607
(813) 874-3918

GEORGIA
Babette Broussard, President
1951 Greystone Road
Atlanta, GA 30318
(404) 256-1232

HAWAII
Jane Anderson and Susan Kowen, Co-Pres.
Ph. Cont.: Jane Anderson
P.O. Box 61610
Honolulu, HI 96839-1610
(808) 538-7007

ILLINOIS
Rosemary White, President
Geraldine Dansky, Executive Director
751 Roosevelt Road
Bldg. 7, Suite 301
Glen Ellyn, IL 60137
(630) 469-6900

INDIANA
Phyllis Hutson and Julia Richter, Co-Pres.
1010 E. 86th Street, Suite 65F
Indianapolis, IN 46240
(765) 844-4259

IOWA
Marlin Geisler, President
1155 330th Street
Box 50A
Gowrie, IA 50543
(515) 352-3548

ISRAEL
David Finkelstein, Pres.
P.O. Box 6309
HOD HASHARON
45240 Israel
972 9 7403160

KANSAS
C. Wilson Anderson, Jr.
Contact
2812 S. W. Osborn
Topeka, KS 66614
(785) 228-1717

LOUISIANA
Marqua Brunette, President
2125 Coliseum Street
New Orleans, LA 70130-5115
(504) 566-7800

MARYLAND
Jean-Fryer Schedler, Pres.
P.O. Box 984
Severna Park, MD 21146
(410) 825-2881

MICHIGAN
Mary Lee Killingbeck, President
2829 W. Grand River Ave., Suite D
Howell, MI 48843
(517) 548-0047

MISSISSIPPI
Billie Hill, President
P.O. Box 2485
Laurel, MS 39442
(601) 428-0857

NEBRASKA
Jennifer Forbes, President
P.O. Box 6302
Lincoln, NE 68506
(402) 486-2506

NEW ENGLAND AREA
(CT, ME, MA, NH, RI, VT)
Lorna Kaufman, President
Kaufman Educational Assoc.
277 Auburn Street
West Newton, MA 02166
(617) 964-4485

NEW JERSEY
Carol King and Judy Shapiro, Co-Pres.
Box 32
Long Valley, NJ 07853
(908) 879-0466

NEW YORK
Buffalo Branch
Linda Clark, President
4625 Harlem Road
Snyder, NY 14226
(716) 839-2918

New York Branch
Stanley Antonoff, President
Iris Spano, Exec. Dir.
71 West 23rd Street, Suite 1500
New York, NY 10010
(212) 691-1930

Suffolk Branch
Michelle Delaney, President
728 Route 25A
Northport (Long Isl.), NY 11768
(516) 261-7441

NORTH CAROLINA
Rebecca Clingman, Pres.
4511 Chinaberry Lane
Winston-Salem, NC 27106
(919) 243-8843

OHIO
Central Ohio Branch
Jane Ashby, President
Marburn Academy
1860 Walden Drive
Columbus, OH 43229
(614) 899-5711

Northern Ohio Branch
Joyce Hedrick, President
177 Glen Road
Chagrin Falls, OH 44022
(216) 556-0883

Ohio Valley Branch
Isabelle Radock, Pres.
317 E. 5th Street
Cincinnati, OH 45202
(513) 651-4747

OKLAHOMA
Joanne S. Corney, Cont.
301 Country Club Circle
Midwest City, OK 73110
(405) 732-1159

OREGON
Lynetta Weswig, President
P.O. Box 3677
Portland, OR 97208
(503) 774-9554

PENNSYLVANIA
Thomas Jennings, President
P.O. Box 251
Bryn Mawr, PA 19010
(610) 527-1548

PUGET SOUND BRANCH
(AK, ID, MT, SD, WA)
Sandi Olsen, President
12020 SE 281st Court
Kent, WA 98031
(206) 382-1020

SOUTH CAROLINA
Felicia Robbins, President
303 Camellia Lane
Simpsonville, SC 29681
(803) 772-8065

SOUTHWEST AREA
(NM, W. TX)
Meg Porch, President
P.O. Box 25891
Albuquerque, NM 87125
(505) 255-8234

TENNESSEE
East Tennessee Branch
Margaret Smith, President
190 Woodcliff Circle
Signal Mountain, TN 37377
(423) 769-0770

West/Middle Tennessee Branch
Rosemary Williams, Pres.
2679 Kingham Drive
Memphis, TN 38119
(901) 754-1441

TEXAS
Austin Branch
Judy Butler, President
11506 Queens Way
Austin, TX 78759
(512) 452-7658
Web: http://www.inetport.com/~dyslexia/austin.html

Dallas Branch
Susan Fleming, President
c/o 4020 McEwen, Ste. 105
Dallas, TX 75244-5019
(214) 357-4714

Houston Branch
Carole Wills, President
P.O. Box 540504
Houston, TX 77254-0504
(713) 529-1975

UPPER MIDWEST AREA
(MN, ND, SD)
Bonnie Berquist, President
8579 Bower Court East
Inver Grove Hts., MN 55076
(H) (612) 450-1043
(W) (612) 699-2442

VIRGINIA
Ann Hicks, President
Ph. Cont.: Ruth Lund
6 Menife Court
Williamsburg, VA 23188
(800) 988-8336

WISCONSIN
William Kitz and Nira Scherz-Busch, Co-Pres.
1317 Washington Avenue
Oshkosh, WI 54901
(414) 299-0551

BRANCH COUNCIL CHAIR
Nancy Hennessy
3 Falcon Lane
Long Valley, NJ 07853
(908) 813-1895

The Learning Disabilities Association of America
4156 Library Road
Pittsburgh, PA 15234
(412) 341-1515 or (713) 774-6405

The British Dyslexia Association
Web site: http://www.bda-dyslexia.org.uk

For Further Reading

Standard Texts

Critchley, Macdonald. *The Dyslexic Child* (Springfield, IL: Charles C. Thomas, 1970). Dr. Critchley, the British authority, began his work at approximately the same time as Samuel T. Orton. He is the source of the information on King Karl XI of Sweden in my text.

Herman, Knud. *Reading Disability: A Medical Study of Word-Blindness and Related Handicaps* (Copenhagen: Munksgaard, 1959). Dr. Herman, the Danish authority, devotes a chapter to anonymous autobiographical accounts, from which I quote.

Jansky, J. J. and de Hirsch, K. *Preventing Reading Failure: Prediction, Diagnosis, Intervention* (New York: Harper and Row, 1972).

Orton, Samuel T. *Reading, Writing, and Speech Problems in Children and Selected Papers* (Baltimore, MD: The Orton Dyslexia Society, 1989). This is the basic text, published in 1937, with additional papers and an introduction by Dr. Richard L. Masland.

Rawson, Margaret Byrd. *The Many Faces of Dyslexia* (Baltimore, MD: The Orton Dyslexia Society, Monograph No. 5, 1988).

Readings for Educators. The Reprint Series. (Baltimore, MD: The Orton Dyslexia Society).

Reading for Parents.

Popular Reprints by the Orton Society

Cicci, Regina. *Dyslexia: Especially for Parents*. 1987 Annals.

Cohen, Jonathan. *Learning Disabilities and Psychological Development in Childhood and Adolescence*. 1986 Annals.

Ellis, William. *The School and the Dyslexic — Mutually Exclusive?* 1986 Annals.

Galaburda, Albert M. *Ordinary and Extraordinary Brain Development: Anatomical Variation in Developmental Dyslexia*. 1989 Annals.

——. *Developmental Dyslexia: Current Anatomical Research*. 1983 Annals.

Gallagher, J. Roswell. *Can't Spell, Can't Read*. Reissued by the Orton Dyslexia Society, Baltimore, MD 21204. Originally published in 1948.

Masland, Richard L., M.D. *The Advantages of Being Dyslexic*. 1976 Bulletin.

Vail, Priscilla L. *Gifts, Talents, and the Dyslexias: Wellsprings, Springboards, and Finding Foley's Rocks*. 1990 Annals.

DATE DUE

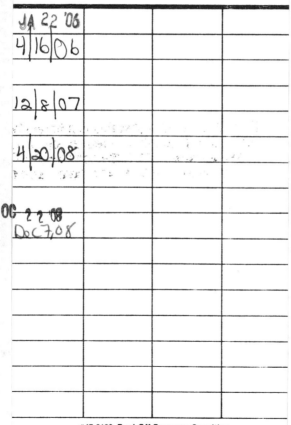

JA 22 '06			
4/16/06			
12/8/07			
4/20/08			
OC 22 08 DEC 7 08			

#47-0108 Peel Off Pressure Sensitive